DRINKS, DRUGS, BIRDS & BOXING VOLUME 2

Ben Doughty

Copyright © 2020 Ben Doughty

All rights reserved

No part of this book may be reproduced, or stored in a retrieval system, or transmitted in any form or by any means, electronic, mechanical, photocopying, recording, or otherwise, without express written permission of the publisher.

ISBN-: 9798696176680

Edited by Natalie Bleau

Cover design by: Ben Doughty & Julian McGowan
Library of Congress Control Number: 2018675309
Printed in the United States of America

To my beautiful sons, Joseph and Lucas, in the hope they may avoid much of the folly contained herein.

1/ IT WAS GOOD OF YOU TO COME

I woke up and hoped it was still Christmas. I pulled back the curtains, by way of investigation, and studied the lamp lit dark for tell tale signs of chronology. But there were none. I walked into the front room and turned the light on. According to the old brass alarm clock on the mantelpiece, it was just after ten past eight in the evening. Surely I couldn't have slept for 33 hours...? It had to be still Christmas.

Jumping in and out of the bath, I picked out the freshest clothes I could find in my bag and scurried up the road to pay Andy and Emma a surprise visit. I was the prodigal son and I had returned. Arriving at Lichfield Court, I pressed the doorbell and heard Emma shriek as she glimpsed the identity of the late night caller through the spy hole.

"OH MY GOD....!"

She opened the door and we shared a hug as Blade came traipsing into the hallway, cheerfully pissed and stoned, as well he might have been.

"Ben, man...! How's it going....?"

He proffered a beer and offered me the leftovers of wild goose or some other such outlandish poultry that had clearly constituted Christmas dinner. With Blade, it was all about avoiding normal life and turkey at Christmas would have been unforgivably plebeian. I said yes to alcohol and no to solid sustenance. I had anecdotes to relay and eating would merely have impeded that process. I needed them both to understand that I had left last summer as a boy but returned on the Messiahs' birthday, a man.

Actually, I didn't care to admit that I hadn't had the pleasure of one single, solitary American girl in my absence or even come especially close. I wasn't about to actively lie but they were welcome to assume the opposite on account of my wanton swagger. And surely I was due plaudits, being gone for 5 months on a measly travel budget of 400 quid...?

As we nestled in the alcove beneath the elevated double bed, Blade conceded that he was impressed. Nonetheless, he censured me for the washing powder passed off as cocaine episode. He shook his head gravely. "That is NOT cool.... If someone had fixed that up they would have died..."

'If someone had fixed that up...?' Obviously, I'd heard about intravenous drug use but it had never occurred to me that shooting up cocaine was a valid recreational activity. I thought that was heroin. Having popped my narcotic cherry, I was hungry for new chemical delights but sticking a needle in myself held no appeal at the time.

The subject of Chris and the fall out was duly addressed. By Andy's account he had been livid and aghast when he returned to London, scarcely able to believe he had been 'so insulted.' I was many years away from acquiring the kind of empathy that was needed in order to realise that I had been a tad ungracious. I figured we'd patch things up.

Before I hit the road, we watched a couple of episodes of the new Harry Enfield series that he had recorded on VHS while I was away. Beer and laughter flowed. After months of exile in the Mountain West, the sheer Englishness of it all hit me in the gut. As had everything else I had experienced in the last 16 hours since landing back in Blighty. It was the closest thing I could admit to a patriotic sensation.

When it came time for me to leave, Andy saw me to the door and we said goodnight. As I walked up Sheen Road, the old stomping ground, I believed myself to be on the cusp of some fabulous new dawn. The 90s would be my defining decade. Of that much I was certain. Having just returned from Boulder - a pastiche of the late 60s - London seemed so much fresher and sharper. The New Year couldn't come soon enough.

I spent Boxing Day watching TV and catching up with friends on the blower, shamelessly bragging about my exploits across the pond. The gigs, the girls, the drugs, the scams.

"So you've been doing lots of shagging...?" Drac tentatively supposed.

"Well... A bit..." I mumbled, vaguely irritated by the bluntness of his enquiry. "But in any case, there's just so much POTENTIAL for an English guy out there..... And you've got to try acid,"

Quite why I would make such a hearty recommendation remained a mystery, since my first experiment had nearly gotten me stabbed and the second debacle had placed me on the verge of permanent mental derangement. With friends like me, a man wouldn't want for enemies.

As I went through my inventory of people to call, continual remarks were made as to how my accent had changed. As ludicrous as it was after a 5 month sojourn, I was proud to have garnered an American brogue. It was almost certainly an affectation but such things were not unprecedented. Dennis Andries had begun to sound like Thomas Hearns as soon as he hit the Detroit tarmac, for example. It's just a shame that he couldn't fight like Tommy,

At 9.15 am on December 27, Dad stumbled through the door swathed in that god awful shell suit with a strange absence of luggage. I already knew the story, more or less. Predictably, he'd gotten slaughtered on Christmas Day and alienated himself from the general ambience of Mum's seasonal gathering. "He RUINED Christmas for everyone," she would later tell me with characteristic melodrama. Consequently, he was banished early doors the next morning with instructions not to darken the doorstep anytime soon. The sensible thing would have been to catch the earliest coach available but alcoholics don't do the sensible thing. So instead, he went on the piss in Chester, had a fight and lost his rucksack. Catching a bit of 'shut eye' on a bench in the city centre, he had jumped on the first coach bound for London at the crack of dawn.

As ever, he found the whole thing hilarious. It always was, so long

as he could maintain the buzz and stay one step ahead of the dire emotional crash that awaited. He looked me up and down for any noticeable aesthetic differences since we had last been in the same room and suggested, "We might as well go to Waitrose and get some cans."
An excellent suggestion, admittedly. And how I loved him for suggesting it.

As we walked down the street, he opined that my gait had changed. Before I left for the States, it had been more camp and contrived, he said. We breezed into Waitrose and he picked up an 8 pack of own brand lager which was comically confused at the check out with the shopping and effects of the old lady in front. Judging by the old dear's reproachful glare, she appeared to hold us personally responsible for the misunderstanding. It was good to be back in Jolly Old England.

Aside from Mike Tyson's cursory dismissal of Alex Stewart 3 weeks earlier, I hadn't seen any boxing throughout my entire stateside jaunt. I'd even missed Evander Holyfield's coronation as Buster Douglas paid the price for the textbook folly of leading with a right uppercut. But news had reached me of Nigel Benn being shorn of his WBO middleweight crown by a cocky young upstart named Chris Eubank.

Back at the flat, libations in hand, Dad inserted the tape into the video recorder. Unfolding on the screen was a bona fide classic as two gladiators, embroiled in that perfect dichotomy of mutual disdain and absolute respect, went back and forth for 26 minutes and 56 seconds in a seismic battle of wills. It was all over in the 9th round as Richard Steele inserted himself between the combatants and cradled a browbeaten Benn in his arms to spare him from further bombardment.

It served as a reminder that everything else in life is essentially inferior to the poetry and majesty of the squared circle. Please don't forget that because I won't.

2/ HARRY THE GROWLER

Eubank made his first defence against a Canadian fighter called Dan Sherry on the 23rd of February, 1991, almost 3 weeks after my 21st birthday. Sherry, whose clipped handsome visage said real estate broker more than prize fighter, was undefeated but largely unknown. His manager was the altogether more illustrious Sugar Ray Leonard. Dad had gotten wind that Sherry might be spending his final fortnight of preparation at the legendary Thomas A' Becket gym on the old Kent Road. 'The Becket' was an iconic British Boxing institution and had hosted innumerable legends of the ring, including Ali and Frazier, since the inception of the small gym above the pub after which it was named in the 1940s.

It seemed reasonable to assume that a world title challenger would have his manager around him in the last days of readying for war. If there was even the slightest chance that our mutual hero could be found within a 5 mile radius of the Becket in the next several days then we'd have cheerfully pitched a tent on the corner of Albany Road. Nonetheless, I had a more practical suggestion.
I would dust off my kit and have a workout at the gym. Dad was no coach but he could hold pads after a fashion and it would give us a legitimate reason to be there whilst not resembling a pair of autograph hunters. We were known at the Becket, in any case, having been frequent visitors over the years.

At the time of our last acquaintance, ex - Southern Area bantamweight champion, Gary Davidson, had been the 'guvnor' but Billy Aird had taken over since then. A former British and European title challenger who had fought a young John Conteh, Billy was a mostly affable scouser, although Dad saw him as a 'lugubrious sod' who always seemed to be locking horns with someone, be it a fighter or the Board of Control.

Mid afternoons had always been peak time for the big names in the 80s so we caught the Tube from Richmond and rolled up to the gym at 2pm on a Wednesday. As we filed up the familiar staircase and through the postage stamp sized gym to the changing room at the back, roughly half a dozen fighters were going through their paces. Shadow boxing, skipping, artfully pummelling the bags or doing groundwork on the designated patterned rugs. No sparring was in progress and there was no sign of Sherry or his entourage.

Having got changed, I began to limber up in the big mirror on the wall opposite the 14 foot ring with just a modicum of self consciousness. I hadn't trained in 2 and a half years and the nature of my sabbatical had not been healthy. Amongst the assorted gym rats, the first person I recognised was Harry Burgess, a Lewisham based manager and promoter, affectionately known as 'Harry The Growler.' He was a stout man in his 60s with grey hair, perpetually obscured by a trademark trilby. I feinted and threw jabs, waiting for him to recognise me.

I didn't know the story behind his moniker but Harry was that archetypal London fight figure who had spent the best part of his middle age lurking in the gym, waiting for that one kid to walk through the door who would change his life forever. The closest he had come hitherto was with a fighter called Alan Lamb but when the 'Lancaster Lion' tumbled shy in a bid for Clinton McKenzie's domestic light welterweight crown in 1983, any dreams of world domination disintegrated.

Throughout my regular visits to the gym as a teenager, Harry had taken a benign interest in my progress. It was he who had taught me to throw the left hook at 45 degrees/ palm facing as opposed to the more amateurish delivery I had previously favoured. As the 3 minute bell rang he walked into my proximity and asked, "Alright, Son…? What you been up to…?"

"Running round America, fucking myself up, H…!" I replied, still dancing and firing combinations.

"Gawd…! You ain't been on the old 'Bob Hope' have you…?" he cackled.

After 3 rounds in the mirror, I donned the mitts for a bit of bag work. As strange as it may sound, there were only 2 punch bags in the gym, despite the large number of professional fighters who often trained at the same time in the condensed house of pain. I'd not done half a round when Harry interjected his sagely wisdom.

"Stop for a second," he commanded.
"I bet you've never knocked anyone out...?"

"I've stopped a few," I assured him.

"Ok, you've stopped a couple but I bet you've never knocked anyone spark out..?"

"No," I admitted.

"Of course you ''avent. 'Cos you're bouncing all over the gaff. 100 miles an hour. Now settle down, hold your feet and throw that 1-2 for me again."

Without bouncing, I did as he asked and my revised execution of boxing's most fundamental combo met with his approval.

"That's better...! Do it again... And again... Now you're talking....!" He turned to the old man, "See...? He's a DEVASTATING puncher when he sits down on that right hand."

I couldn't help thinking his assessment was a tad hyperbolic and I took little pleasure in hearing it. It may seem quaint to the layman but I didn't want compliments on my power. I desired to be appreciated for my speed and finesse. I was only here in the first place because I wanted to meet Sugar Ray Leonard.

"Brian, take him on the pads," ordered Harry. Brian was the coach to whom he entrusted the honing of his various fistic protégés and, presumably, it was a quiet day for such things. I stepped into the ring and he duly gave me 4 rounds of blood, sweat and tears, stopping only to correct any perceived imperfections. After months of idle decadence, my fitness was pretty woeful but I got through the ordeal with stoicism whilst feeling that I had rather lost control of the afternoon's agenda. As the ad hoc session concluded, Harry looked at me before looking at Brian. "What d'ya

reckon…?"
Clearly more parsimonious with compliments, Brian conceded, "Yeah, he's got a nice jab."

Harry cut to the chase. "There's plenty of sparring for you but if you want that you've gotta' come and work with me and Brian everyday at 2 O' Clock. It constituted an unexpected turn of events but I heard myself saying, "Ok, let's do it."
I was flattered by the attention and the notion that the 'magic' was still there. Brian gave me some groundwork before I hit the shower. Perhaps it was the hand of fate and I was destined for ring glory after all.

I turned up the next day with the old man in tow at the agreed hour. I did another 4 rounds on the pads with Brian plus all the trimmings, including some partnered callisthenics with a black light heavyweight hopeful called Robert. As I grunted my way through some excruciating sit ups, he offered a motivational maxim:

"If it ain't hurtin' ya then it ain't doing ya' no good is it…?"

Robert worked as a nightclub bouncer and had no amateur ring experience but wanted to turn pro all the same. 20 years later the Board would have welcomed him with open arms. On the Friday, as I walked out of the changing room, Harry said, "I was on phone to an amateur club last night about getting you a couple of contests. Shake the rust off." I knew what I was doing when I replied, "I'm not really interested in trophies, Harry. I've got enough already."

"You interested in money, son…?" he asked.

"Yes," I answered.

"That's my man…! How old are you..? 21… If you listen to me, by the time you're 30 you could have enough money to last you the rest of your life."

So there we had it. I was 'turning over' and the old man was enormously excited. At this particular time he was supposed to be enrolled on some sports related vocational course, as directed by the job centre. Now that his dream had been reignited he lost all interest in such tedious frippery. "Who the hell wants to be there when you can be HERE," he asked with appropriate rhetoric. It was such a shame that I was going to let him down.

On the Monday, Brian asked if I had a gum shield. I told him I did. "I thought you could have a move around with Lester today," he said by way of explanation. Lester Jacobs was a middleweight out of Peckham with a 5- 0 record. He claimed to have sparred with Eubank, Benn and Watson and I had no particular reason to doubt him. He would go on to win his next 24 fights on the spin whilst remaining in total obscurity. I got gloved up and borrowed Robert's head guard before ducking between the ropes. I'd shadow boxed innumerable rounds in the famous ring but this would be my first time trading real leather within its confines. Perhaps I should say half real. In accordance with sparring protocol when a bigger fighter moves a smaller fighter around, Lester went easy on me. And when the bigger fighter does that he often looks ponderous and slow in comparison.

For 3 rounds Lester came forward as I danced around him throwing fast combinations, up and down. Some of the shots he blocked but several got through, prompting him to nod in acknowledgement whilst firing back with a measured restraint. If you didn't know what you were watching, it might have appeared that I was boxing rings around him. Or if you were blinded by paternal adoration.

"I don't see how he'd find you, even in a real fight," said Dad, beaming with pride at the conclusion of the 9 minute session.

"Quite impressive, actually.." agreed Harry. "He could make a right few bob because he's white and he can punch."

If I was a puncher then it was news to me but the assembled onlookers, including West Country boxing stalwart, Chris Sanigar, nodded approvingly like converts to Harry's latest cult. 9 short weeks ago, I'd been out of my brain on hallucinogenics in a Colorado campus kitchen. Now I was the Great White Hope of South London.

In the thick of all this excitement, I almost forgot to tell you: Dad's information about Sherry training at the Beckett turned out to be bogus. Wherever he might have trained, the slick Canadian certainly made a total nuisance of himself before collapsing in the 10th round, apparently in dire distress from the effects of an innocuous backward head butt.

Sherry had frustrated Eubank all night long with his superior movement whilst maintaining a constant flow of uncomplimentary verbiage in the champion's direction. In the conclusive round Eubank was coming on strong before being turned on the ropes after which the challenger whispered something in his ear. Eubank claimed it was a racial epithet and duly flicked the back of his head into his tormentor's face as the latter collapsed like a man caught in a hail of bullets.

To this day, Sherry maintains he blacked out due to excessive blood loss from a cut lip sustained early in the fight but Team Eubank and the partisan Brighton crowd were predictably sceptical. Faking or not, with Sherry unable to continue it was decreed that the fight would go to the cards. By any neutral arbitration, it was hard to see how the champion could possibly have been ahead but the split verdict in his favour came as no surprise.

In boxing, the house fighter almost always wins.

3/ NO MAS

Harry said I would make my pro debut at the National Sporting Club in May. Dad was over the moon and Mum was horrified. She didn't like the aimless gallivanting or nagging suspicion that I was au fait with the fringes of the pharmaceutical industry but had at least hoped that any competitive boxing was in the rear view mirror. Between the ages of 11 and 18, I'd had 34 amateur fights and Mum had felt sick on the handful of occasions she attended. The very thought of her first born son being cast into the sewer of professional boxing was even more abhorrent. But she needn't have worried.

The denouement was most inglorious. One afternoon, in the middle of an uncharacteristically sluggish sparring session with an amateur light middleweight, I just walked out of the ring and mouthed "Fuck this.." through the impediment of a gum shield. Quitting without a legitimate reason was the ultimate taboo, sparring or not. Mortified, the old man shouted "GET BACK IN THERE…!" but I ignored him and headed for the changing room.

I slumped on the bench in abject silence and shunned all offers of a tough love pep talk. The kind you might see 3 quarters into a Rocky movie with Adrian busting out home truths on the beach. Dad even tried the Angelo Dundee line, "All we want from you is SIX MINUTES…" But it was to no avail.

The truth is that my heart wasn't in it anymore. Other people wanted this to happen. Not me. I'd just gone along with it out of vanity. I hated hanging out with Andy and Julian while drinking Diet Coke and refusing the spliff or a line of something invigorating. I wanted to live out my Rock n' Roll dreams and America had been a mere hors d'ouvre. Trainers and pugs spoke of 'living the life.' For a young man in his prime it seemed like no life at all so far I was concerned.

Dad took my gloves off and I showered and changed before we both endured a very muted journey home. To this day, I feel wretched about disappointing him like that and wasting everybody's time.

Having shirked the opportunity to fulfil my ring potential, I was free to pick up the dissolute life I had been pursuing for the last 3 years. I knocked about with Andy in the local watering holes and played a lot of guitar whilst attempting to write songs. As my mentor, he explained that writing a song about one's girlfriend was unbearably naff and that an artist should explore dark themes and dysfunctional narratives. So the first song I wrote was a sweet, sardonic ditty about my alcoholic granddad leaving my grandmother to walk to the local boozer in a torrential rainstorm while he took the car. It was called 'She Likes to Walk', with the old man singing harmonies on the makeshift demo tape.

In July, Drac came to visit with a retinue that included his stunning new girlfriend, Jenny. She was a few days shy of her 16th birthday and resembled a brunette Claudia Schiffer with an irresistible smattering of churlish adolescent vitriol. Drac and Jenny had been an item for several months but any potential controversy stemming from the brevity of her summers was probably kept at bay by the sheer womanliness of her visage. He just didn't look like a nonce with her on his arm.

Also present was our mutual friend Alex and her new boyfriend, along with my old mate, Nick. Introductions taken care of, the 6 of us caught the tube to Oxford Circus for the obligatory West End shopping experience. Ticking off the usual ports of call - HMV, Tower Records and Carnaby Street - we finished up at the Intrepid Fox for a swift half. The Fox was a punk/metal hang out but my abiding memory of the joint related to its hosting of the James Kinchen - Buster Drayton weigh in back in 1985. The old man and I had been refused entry because I was underage and we thought it a diabolical liberty.

As the evening approached, it was time to meet Blade at the White Cross back in Richmond. I considered it compulsory that any friends who made the trip to London should make his acquaintance as he was the closest thing I had to a pop cultural V.I.P. Seated on the jetty that was a natural extension of the riverside pub, I waited expectantly for him to regale the assembled company. "Tell them about the time John Lydon squirted you with a Fairy Liquid bottle full of piss because you shagged his bird...."

Blade generally liked the ambience of younger people as they tended to be closer to the romantic idealism that had fuelled his initial rise to 'stardom.' Predictably, he was rather smitten with Jenny. "She's only 15...." I announced. Freshly besotted with her Camden Market splendour and cascading hair, he asked:

"Are you REALLY....?"

"I'll be 16 on Wednesday," she replied with casual disinterest.

It was time for more drinks and Drac offered to get them in, retaining Aly to provide assistance with the conveyance of our various tipples. Aly was Alex's boyfriend and he and Drac had gotten increasingly close since my absence from the old town. Only a year older than Jenny, he was a prodigious rock drummer with flowing dark locks and 80 percent of Archway School's fifth form girls were said to be in love with him. Drac had been with Aly on the night he met Jenny and it transpired that he had also taken my advice about the desirability of LSD. They both agreed that their first 'trip' several weeks ago had been 'a riot.'

Although my two previous experiences had been rather harrowing, I was desperate for another taste of the fabled psychedelic now that I was back on home soil. To that end, Drac said that acid was copiously available in Stroud, along with various other narcotic staples. It didn't sound like the Stroud I remembered but I was happy to take his word for it. Andy smoked a fair bit of hash and his mate, Simeon, usually had coke but he wasn't indulging at the kind of pace that I was looking for at this stage. He was 9 years older and married, after all. Keen to take advantage of Stroud's black economy, I made a pact to visit the following weekend. I was looking forward to getting high as a kite in the agrarian valleys of my childhood and asked for a show of hands. Still sober due to imminent driving duties and naturally conservative at the best of times, Nick said he was up for it and I could stay at his parents' house.

As we drank up and said our farewells, he can't have known the extent to which he would regret such enthusiasm in 7 days time.

4/ JENNIFER JUNIPER

The following Friday lunchtime, I ventured to the trusty old lay by near the Lucozade factory in Chiswick and waited for a lift. In the first half of the 90s, it was anathema to pay for trains when I could simply stick my thumb out. That was how desperados got around and I felt sorry for anyone who didn't understand that.

I was making good progress, having reached the A419 in a couple of hours, when I was picked up by a gangly Welsh bloke in a battered white Cortina. I couldn't help noticing that either he or someone else had seen fit to obscure the front and rear number plates with hastily applied masking tape. It seemed odd but I didn't suppose it was any of my business. On further inspection, I could see that the car didn't seem to fit him at all well. The driver's seat was lodged very close to the steering wheel causing his knees to protrude at an angle of 45 degrees, almost touching his chin. He seemed jittery, like a man at the tail end of a Dexedrine bender.

"I nicked this car," he confessed after a few minutes silence. "Oh really..?" I replied, not knowing what else to say. Having got that off his chest, he went on to explain that he had also done a runner from a petrol station about 8 miles up the road and hadn't paid for the fuel that was currently propelling us South West. Presumably, that accounted for the masking tape.

Becoming his unwitting accomplice constituted an unwelcome development but the advent of speed cameras and CCTV was still a couple of years away and panic was unlikely to achieve anything. I was more concerned he might crash the vehicle before the law caught up with us. At this point, he hadn't said where he was going or how far he could take me. As it happened, the matter was taken out of his hands before too long.

As we neared Cirencester, thick black smoke began to billow from the bonnet as the car radically slowed against the driver's volition. A vaguely loud bang emanated from the source of the smoke, eliciting the word, "FUCK...!" from my lanky new sidekick. He pulled onto the hard shoulder as we disembarked from the smoking wreck and took stock of the surrounding terrain. "Sorry, mate, all the best," he offered before straddling a fence and sprinting across the adjacent field into the distance. I was on my own.

The first priority was to get away from the scene of the crime. I figured that Kemble Station couldn't be too far away so I trudged across the field in search of road signs and provincial civilisation. My instinct proved to be good, although it was an hour's walk at anyone's pace. I arrived at the station and waited for the next train to Stroud, one stop away. I wouldn't be needing a ticket as there were no barriers at either end, although there might be an inspector on the train. I would cross that bridge if I came to it. Hitching was analogous to life, I thought. There will always be forks in the road but you will reach your destination with determination and belief.

The Great Western Railway service pulled into Stroud at just after 5pm. I sought the nearest pay phone and gave Nick a call. I still knew the number off by heart from the days when I briefly terrorised the family with nuisance calls. You can blame that on adolescent boredom in the pre internet era. He picked up within a couple of rings and I asked him to meet me in the town centre and to let Drac know of our plans.

Half an hour later, the three of us met in the Pelican as it was by far the best bet for anyone looking to score recreational drugs. In the 80s, I remembered it as more of a lad's pub, bristling with violence, but it had since become the town's epicentre of alternative culture. A haven for hippies, punks, ravers, goths and the dreadful burgeoning phenomenon of the 'New Age Traveller.'

We sat near the pool table as Drac asked various bohemian looking acquaintances if anyone was holding any 'trips.' In an effort to assert their street credibility, some of them alluded to imminent shipments from Bristol, Bath or Timbuktu but the short answer was that they couldn't help us. We tried the Vic, which was also patronised by 'heads' and unemployed visionaries but there was nothing doing.

The pressure was on Drac, having boasted that my old home town was such a hotbed of illegal stimulants in the first place. "We could try Woody…" he suggested. I agreed that it wasn't a bad idea. Rob Wood had been a couple of years below us at school and was one of those trendy 'cutting edge' types, always on the latest youth cultural bandwagon. At school I had regarded him as a cool guy although he would become an insufferable presence over the next several months.

As we reached Woody's parents' house on Langtoft Road (the same street on which Drac lived at the top of town) the visible tie dye print on his bedroom wall seemed like a good omen. We rang the doorbell and asked if Rob was home. Summoned by his lovely Iraqi mother, he appeared in the doorway wearing a hooded top emblazoned with some kind of drug culture reference.

"Have you got any acid…?" we asked in unison.

"Funnily enough, I have….!" he confirmed.

There was a story attached to this fortuitous turn of events to which I payed little attention. The important thing was that Rob had 6 tabs of acid for sale, each baring a red dragon emblem. He wanted 20 quid for the lot, which seemed fair enough. Nick gave him a £20 note in exchange for the goods and Drac and I promised to sort him out later.

Another old school mate who lived on Langtoft Road was Neil, only just returned from a 3 year stint at Lancaster University. Being as we had 6 tabs and there were only 3 of us, it seemed polite to ask if he cared to join us for the evening. Most of our peer group had just completed 36 months of further education in various parts of the UK and you didn't know who might be into drugs and who had remained straight laced. None of us had been into drugs during the sixth form years, so all the pamphlets and melodramatic videos had been wasted. It transpired that Neil was on nodding terms with narcotics and was only too delighted to tag along. The four of us walked back to Drac's house just as Jenny arrived in a taxi, sporting denim shorts and a scant maroon top beneath a black leather jacket.

It was decreed that Jenny couldn't partake of any Class As as she was as only 16 and still at school. By way of a surrogate, we dropped into an off license on Parliament Street and purchased her a bottle of cheap red wine on the way back into town. It was a cool summer evening and the undulating greenery that surrounded the shops and houses loomed large and beautiful.
Trudging down the steep incline, we paused momentarily, allowing everyone besides Jenny to wash down the small square tabs of impending lunacy with a communal bottle of diet cola. Acid typically takes half an hour to an hour before the user experiences any effects. The question was, who would come up first…? The unpredictability was part of the excitement.

We walked past the Silver Rooms arcade where Drac once got nicked for smashing a fruit machine and into the pedestrianised area that constituted the central business district. As we approached the bridge that links the bus station to Beeches Green, Aly and Alex could be seen seated on a bench at the foot of Slad Road. They appeared to be embroiled in a serious discussion - quite at odds with our vibe - and gave the impression of desiring to be alone when we briefly engaged them in conversation.

We continued up Slad Road and into the rural yonder, waiting for visual evidence of the drug's efficacy. A giant malevolent Twix wrapper, perhaps, or a tree transmuted into a dinosaur. Dusk gave way and night seemed to fall as radically as if some celestial stage hand had suddenly drawn a black velvet curtain encrusted with stars. As my confederates pressed on, Jenny and I hung back and got to know each other.

"Why did Andy say he loved me the other night..?" she wanted to know.

"Blade…? It's just the kind of thing he says to a pretty girl. He's a poet after all." I explained.

The bottle being half finished, she was flirtatiously drunk by now. .She moved closer and seemed to invite my arm to encircle her waist. I could feel the acid kicking in. "Who's that with their arm around Jenny...?" Drac shouted, 50 odd yards ahead of our conjoined silhouettes. His tone was jocular, as if to say, 'I'm watching you but I'm ok with it.' Perhaps regarding it as a tacit seal of approval we were soon getting off with each other, our mouths locked in the timeless ritual of carnal foreplay. Snogging one's best mates' girlfriend on LSD within his partially obscured sight. Was it acceptable...? I gave myself an instant pass. If we were to embrace the drugs of the 'flower power' generation then surely we should assimilate the values of free love, no possessions and all that jazz. It made perfect sense to me.

Within a couple of minutes, we disengaged from the clinch and caught up with the others as the group converged to compare notes. Suddenly, it became graphically apparent that Nick, the acid virgin, was having a bad trip. There was no talking to the lad and he seemed not to recognise any of us. Apparently frozen with fear, he sprawled on a grass verge at the side of the road like a tremulous field mouse on an airport runway. Drac attempted a benign intervention.

"NICK, I REALLY WANT YOU TO HAVE A GOOD TIME....!" he said slowly, in the manner of a friendly psychiatric nurse. There was a brief glimmer of hope when Nick identified the form standing over him as 'that ugly bastard' but it proved to be no more than a brief spasm of coherence. "Do me a favour and give Nick a kiss," Drac said to Jenny. Het auburn mane spilled onto his petrified countenance as she leaned forward and engaged in what looked like a first aid C.P.R demonstration on a latex dummy. Despite her admirable commitment to the new polygamy, it apparently did nothing to extricate Nick from his abject private hell. If anything, it made things worse. Perhaps he thought an inverted Medusa was plunging her soft serpentine flesh into the depths of his soul. He certainly wasn't betraying any normal reaction to a hot chick's dutiful advances.

Subsequent events remain unaccounted for but must have encompassed several hours. The dawn broke without warning and Jenny seemed to vanish as the sun came up over the hills, exposing our ragged pale faces and dilated pupils. It turned out that she had left in a taxi bound for Painswick several hours ago but, in ignorance of that fact, I thought we might genuinely have lost her. I could see that we were walking back towards the town, as vehicles passed by intermittently.

Nick was still refusing to utter a single solitary word and proceeded with a stoop that caused me to suggest he was carrying our collective sins. On reflection, it was an insensitive thing to say and can't have helped. Like the four horsemen of the apocalypse minus their integral steeds, we walked 2 miles to Cashes Green where Nick's family had moved a few years previously Outside the Village Post Office, where my first serious squeeze had once lived, Nick's mum suddenly ambled into view, driving a Renault 5 with his baby sister in the back. Horrifyingly, she stopped the car in order to talk us:

"Morning....! Where've you lot been..? Out on the tiles...?"

It was 7am and she looked cheerfully demonic. For his part, Nick stared at her the way one might stare at a child molester in the dock. He didn't seem to acknowledge any previous acquaintance. I made my best attempt at small talk in an effort to divert her attention from the plain evidence that her son was hopelessly addled, in a way that simply had to be illegal. Strangely, she didn't appear to notice anything amiss and was soon on her way, cooing, "Have fun, boys.."

We attempted to enter Nick's house via the back garden but, unfortunately, his Dad opened the kitchen door and immediately sensed that all was not well. "NICKLUS....?!"
He eyed his eldest son suspiciously before switching his gaze to the rest of us and back again. 'Say something, you silly cunt...!' I thought. But 'Nicklus' stood stock still and said NOTHING.

"He's had too much Southern Comfort..." I offered weakly, deciding that only Southern Comfort could plausibly induce this kind of rigid catatonic funk. Clive was naturally sceptical.

"Are you sure he hasn't touched anything else....?"

"Not so far I know. And we've been with him all night," I promised.

He didn't appear to believe us but neither did he want to believe the alternative. Drac and Neil made their excuses leaving me to face the music. "We'd best get him to bed," said Clive. I agreed that it was a capital idea. We filed up the stairs of their semi detached home and I endured the further ordeal of helping his father blow up an inflatable mattress for me to 'sleep' on. As the three of us manhandled the finished product into Nick's tiny room, it was excruciatingly hard not to laugh.

Nick climbed under his duvet, fully clothed as 'Clive asked once more, "Are you sure he's ok...?"
"He'll be fine," I said, reclining on the makeshift bed and willing him to shut the door and leave us alone. Mercifully, he did so. Suddenly, Nick opened his eyes and spoke actual words, as if to prove he hadn't entirely lost the facility.

"I had a really weird dream last night," he said "I was carrying everyone's sins and Jenny was kissing me for some reason."

I reached up and pulled back the duvet, inviting him to realise that he was still wearing his black jeans and Aerosmith T - Shirt. Presented with the evidence that it hadn't been a nightmare after all, he looked at me in earnest.

"Please tell me ONE thing. I didn't eat insects did I...?"

"Not so far as I'm aware," I admitted. "Wait a second, do we have another tab left...? We bought 6 and Drac kept 1, right...?"

"If we do then you're welcome to it.." he replied before rolling over and submerging his head under the quilt. In fairness, I should probably have guessed that he wasn't going to fight me tooth and nail for it.

5/ YOU LOVE US

On August 12, 1991 Drac and I went to see Manic Street Preachers at the Hibernian with Blade. Rolling up on Mount Ararat Road in his trusty beige car, he had also brought a matchbox full of acid in order to maximise the profundity of the experience. 'The Manics' were the new darlings of the hip music press who had fallen for their glam punk aesthetic and vitriolic diatribes alongside a promise to take over the universe or crawl back into the sick, inbred hole from which they had emerged.

They had yet to release a debut album but the singles 'Motown Junk' and 'You Love Us' titillated the indie crowd and the rock kids in equal measure. 3 months earlier, band chief spokesman, androgynous pinup and semi competent rhythm guitarist, Richey Edwards, had made his mark quite literally when he carved the slogan '4 REAL' into his forearm during a post gig interview with Steve Lamaq. He was hospitalised, requiring 17 stitches but his gleeful punk rock nihilism was a welcome antidote to the shoe gazing dirge that had pervaded the scene in recent years.

Richey was quoted as saying that he hated 'Slowdive' more than Hitler. I'd never actually heard 'Slowdive' but, instinctively, I agreed with him. Blade was already an aloof elder statesman but Drac and I needed something home-grown and current to throw our allegiance behind. Perhaps these bombastic boys from Blackwood might fit the bill.

After fixing our hair and applying the obligatory eyeliner, we each swallowed half a tab .Our conservatism was based on the logic that half a trip would enhance our perception of the show without placing us in a potentially perilous situation surrounded by pogoing punk parodies.
Although he wouldn't be coming to the gig, Dad took a whole hit himself. He wasn't really the drugs type, under his own steam, but never seemed shy of introducing foreign substances to his bloodstream if anyone was offering. I suppose anything was preferable to his default emotional settings. I had my doubts about the wisdom of him tripping in the flat on his own whilst sat in front of

the regular blizzard of mind numbing soap operas but he was a grown man, when all said and done. We said we'd be back around midnight.

Taking the short walk around the corner, we met Blade outside Lichfield Court and continued towards the station. He insisted we stop at Threshers, so he could purchase a half bottle of cheap whisky, which he duly poured into a silver hip flask.

"Are you not getting anything...?" he asked.

"We're tripping," I told him. "Took a half 10 minutes ago."

He looked vaguely troubled at the implicit lack of altered state symmetry but it wasn't as if he had a leg to stand on in terms of disapproval. I'd heard too many tales of his LSD soaked nights at The Roxy or the Roundhouse back in the day. We hopped on the District Line to Earl's Court, changing there for a Wimbledon service to Fulham Broadway. En route, Blade took intermittent slugs of Scotch whilst Drac and I waited for the acid to kick in.

With hindsight, it seems fair to say there is little point in taking half portions of lysergic acid diethylamide. It's basically the chemical equivalent of coitus interruptus. After half an hour, everything seems slightly woozy and weird but the peak never comes. Either take it or don't would be my advice. At least we had the consolation of the half dozen tabs we had left back at the flat in Dad's fridge. (Drac had read somewhere that acid should be kept cool.)

As we arrived at the venue, Blade circumvented the queue and mentioned the name of his connection at the Box Office window. We picked up the wrist bands that delineated our inclusion on the guest list and walked through the double doors as some generic hard rock act were finishing their set. If the Manics intended to blow us away then this lot constituted the perfect prelude in their abundant mediocrity.

After a short break, the headline act's intro tape suddenly filled the hall with siren noises and an unknown American monologue. The band took the stage and launched straight into 'You Love Us' without a formal introduction. As Drac and I gravitated to the middle of the mosh pit, Blade kept his distance. The hands on approach was too fannish for a former punk rock star.

'WE WON'T DIE OF DEVOTION
UNDERSTAND WE CAN NEVER BELONG
THROW SOME ACID ON THE MONA-LISA'S FACE
POLLUTE YOUR MINERAL WATER
WITH A STRYCHNINE TASTE'

It takes years to develop a good ear for a band's live sound. Half tripping, I imagined they sounded like something I could plausibly champion but was far from certain. As suspected, Richey was the most camera friendly with his black hair, white jeans, chiffon black shirt and scarf. He even had a frighteningly accurate lookalike in the first row, head banging inches from his idol's feet.

Nicky Wire looked a tad gawky in motion but tumbled on the right side of epicene cool as he bounced around, windmilling a Fender bass and snarling the odd backing vocal in his stencil 'Clash' uniform. James Dean Bradfield was plainly an heroic front man but not the most logistically handsome incumbent pop star. His short stocky frame, curly hair and backwards baseball cap prompted Drac to observe, "He's no cooler than I am….!"

After 5 songs, I needed to liberate myself from the sweaty heaving throng and get Blade's take on all of this. I couldn't trust my half ripped senses and he was the sage after all. Hanging near the bar he caught sight of me and proclaimed "I'm convinced…! The singer may be ugly but he's got stage presence and he can play." He was more than half cut by now and attempting to charm a pair of self confessed lesbians despite their continually stated lack of interest.

The band played for another 20 minutes, closing with 'Motown Junk' in a crescendo of reckless posturing and caterwauling feedback. Suddenly it rained white balloons, each bearing a lipstick kiss and the words 'Stay Beautiful.' Who could fail to love a band that mixed politics with punk and kitsch...?

WE'RE LIVING UP IN HELL.... WE DESTROY ROCK AND ROLL....'

There was no encore but rumours of an after-show party prevented us from heading for the exit. Blade was probably our best bet for gaining admittance but where was he...? I scanned the floor as the crowd began to disperse but his angular form was nowhere to be seen.

Since there was no evidence of security, we ventured backstage and duly found him flanked by 2 identikit punks with Geordie accents, getting stuck into what appeared to be the Manic Street Preachers' rider. He was wasted by now and cut a comical figure, sat on the floor with his new pals, draining a can of Guinness. It would surely have been a demystifying spectacle for any starry eyed autograph hunters who might have chanced upon the scene.

Sean Moore, the shy long haired drummer made a brief appearance and asked, ever so politely, if there was anything left to drink. Blade handed him a can of his own booze for which he seemed absurdly grateful before exiting the room. Predictably, I let it slip to the punks that they were drinking with none other than Andy Blade Esquire, formerly of the seminal 'Eater.' Enthused by this revelation, the elder of the two suggested that if 'X-Ray Spex' and 'Sham 69' were still treading the boards then "Why can't Eata' do it...?" Blade curled his lip contemptuously. "Bollocks.. I'm not part of all that. It's embarrassing." 5 years hence, a £5000 offer to play a weekend nostalgia fest in Blackpool would make an abject liar of him.

The Manic Street Preachers' dressing room was somewhat denuded of charm without their actual presence. Mindful of this, Drac and I left Blade to siphon the dregs of adult beverages and went off in search of the party. The exclusive gathering was being held in an adjacent room to the main hall and a ticket was required to pass the threshold. After an initial knock back from the bouncer, we lucked out when James Dean Bradfield rolled up and told us to walk through with him. For someone who might reasonably have been on a star trip, he seemed very decent and unpretentious.

Unfortunately, the same could not be said for the spurious types who populated the soulless affair. As various personages attempted to look important and curry favour, Drac shot me a glance and said, "Let's go back to Richmond and take loads of drugs." It was a good call, I agreed.

Plucking Andy from his backstage bunker, we got back on the street and realised we had missed the last tube. Borderline paralytic, Blade flagged down a taxi and mumbled, "Richmond, please." We bundled into the cab and I told the driver to head for Mt. Ararat Road. 25 minutes later, when we pulled up outside the flat, it became apparent that Blade didn't have a red cent with which to pay the fare despite having instigated such a costly mode of conveyance. Reluctantly, Drac produced a £20 note and shoved it under the partition.

It had to be around 1am and it suddenly occurred to me that Dad must have been tripping tor several hours by now. I had no idea what to expect as I gingerly opened the street door with my confederates bringing up the rear. The place was in total darkness, so the old man was either in the bedroom or absent from the premises entirely. I went to the kitchen to retrieve the acid from the fridge only to discover that the matchbox was still there but the drugs were conspicuously absent. In their stead was a note that read 'DON'T WORRY IT'S IN SAFE HANDS….'

It didn't look good. Was he simply incapable of doing anything in moderation…? Worst case scenarios began to form as we gravitated towards the bedroom to investigate. I knocked on the door, politely at first but with increased urgency when no response was forthcoming. Soon we were all knocking in unison until Blade solemnly called a halt to the ritual percussion and gravely announced, "I'm afraid this has all the hallmarks of a really heavy trip.."

"I'll GIVE YOU A HEAVY TRIP IN A MINUTE.. YA' NOISY SHOWER O' CRAP….!"

Dad opened the door in his trusty blue bath robe, hairpiece slightly askew but visibly sober and annoyed. The drugs didn't work, he moaned. He'd spent the night in front of the box, waiting for any noticeable hallucinogenic effects before giving up and going to bed. He had confiscated the remaining stash, he explained, to prevent us from the necking the lot upon our return. Going forward, he suggested we all get some sleep and try again in the morning.

The acid wasn't dud. I knew that much from the half doses that Drac and I had taken. I made it abundantly clear that we intended to finish what we'd started and he was perfectly welcome to join us. After balking momentarily about the lateness of the hour, Dad handed back the sheet of strawberry branded squares and ventured to the kitchen to fetch a bottle of lemonade with which to wash them down.

I dimmed the lights and inserted a VHS recording of Yellow Submarine' into the VCR machine. Acid taken on top of acid comes on very quickly and the vivid colours of the 1968 animation classic transported me to an ethereal world of magical possibilities. It was hard to imagine the film being made for any other purpose than to provide the perfect cinematic experience for the supremely drug addled but Dad just stared at the screen as if he might be watching a particularly bland tutorial on the basic tenets of road safety.

"I never really liked this film anyway," he said, tragically oblivious to its brilliance. For whatever reason, he was clearly immune to the stuff and giving him any more would have been tantamount to throwing good money after bad. Perhaps he was on such a glut of industrial strength medication that the LSD simply couldn't find a way through the chemical picket line. At the film's conclusion, he yawned and said he was going to hit the hay.

Alongside such staples as 'never meet your heroes' and 'always think ahead' perhaps we can add 'don't take drugs with your parents' to the checklist of ordinary wisdom.

6/ THE AGONY AND THE ECTASY

By the time September came to pass, I had convinced Mum to allow to me to move back into the family home in Paganhill which had been on the market since they evacuated in 1988. In spite of this own mother's reservations, Drac moved in, too, and called dibs on the master bedroom with the en suite shower. Boasting 4 bedrooms, 3 bathrooms and the surrounding acreage, Brooklands would be our Graceland, we decided. The perfect launch pad for a rock star legacy and a magnet for the chicks.

Within a few days of us taking up residence, the new school term started as Jenny began her lower 6th year at Archway Comprehensive. Consequently, lunch times were soon characterised by regular visits from a gaggle of teenage girls, attracted to the mystique of Jenny's older boyfriend and his mate from London. It was an ego trip to have a ready-made congregation of wide eyed groupies hanging on my every word but most of them were too young to seriously interest me.

On the first available Friday we hosted a house warming party attended by several of Jenny's friends and, for the sake of balance, a few of the sixth form lads. The first hour or so was rather pedestrian but proceedings were considerably spiced up when an attractive young brunette by the name of Stacey took a fancy to the sumptuous beige corner bath in the upstairs bathroom. No doubt aided by a few Cinzanos, she asked if it might be filled with water in order to facilitate a 'communal bath.'

Her request presented a conundrum. We had yet to get the hot water switched back on but there was an electric shower in the en suite adjoining the master bedroom. Spurred by the possibility of naked female flesh, I ran a hose pipe from the shower to the bath and soon had it filled to an acceptable level. By degrees, Stacey and her blonde bobbed friend, Louise, stripped topless and plunged into the freshly warm water. Oblivious to what might be going in the rest of the house, I swiftly joined them in my boxer shorts.

I'd clearly come a long way since the days of collecting American phone numbers. THIS was what Rock Stars did. They lounged in decorous corner baths, flanked by attentive topless girls. Before I could get too vainglorious, Neil suddenly entered the room. Somewhat taken aback by the plain evidence of my good fortune, he exclaimed, "SORRY...!" and was about to leave before the girls insisted, "No... Come and join us...!"

Not wishing to look a gift horse in the mouth, he hastily disrobed and entered the fray. The ratio was now less ideal from my perspective but he was a good looking lad and I could hardly begrudge him his share of the spoils. We made out with the girls on a mix and match basis, interspersing said activity with fleeting visits to the lounge at Stacey's behest, in order to dance to the strains of Jimi Hendrix, The Doors and Hanoi Rocks.

As the young ladies cavorted in their knickers, glistening wet, a few of the 17 year old boys moped on the sidelines, possibly wondering what manner of evil voodoo magic we might be conversant with. I felt a twinge of sympathy for I had once been in their shoes, coming second best to the older dropouts or the guys with cars.

Over the next several weeks, we held regular parties on Friday and Saturday nights, sometimes running into one another in a blur of booze, drugs and adrenaline. The teenage contingent was still in evidence but the gatherings also began to attract some of my older contemporaries from back in the day, including the incongruously named Tabby' and 'Chiggles.' A pair of brothers who like me had trained and boxed out of Roxburgh House ABC in the 80s but now appeared to be the local crime lords.

Ecstasy was all the rage and 'free parties' were the places to be, if you could find them. If we weren't hosting a bash of our own, then we would plot up in The Pelican on a Friday or Saturday evening awaiting word on the rumoured location of an illegal outdoor rave that might be going down anywhere within a 200 mile radius. The process of following the convoy and circumventing police road blocks was vastly more exciting than the events themselves from my perspective. I hated the music and the mandatory argot, not to mention the spurious hero worship of the dispensable twats manning the decks with names like 'DJ Daisy', 'DJ Rainbow' and other such infantile tags.

But I liked the drugs. Consequently, it wasn't unusual for Drac, Neil and myself to undertake a several hundred mile round trip to score a consignment of acid, ecstasy or (on one occasion) ketamine before hurriedly driving back to Paganhill and chilling out to the Rolling Stones. The more I thought about it, the more I was aggrieved that my youth had fallen in this era. The 60s or 70s would have been so much more appropriate.

Despite my loathing for techno, trance, happy hardcore and 'blips', I would sometimes endure these wretched affairs until the sun rose and the 'high tunes' came on. Frequently, I might find myself in the back of a random Ford Capri with some temporarily reformed football hooligan with whom I'd had a ruck at school, declaring his colossal love and respect for me. Sadly, there was no depth to it.

The first time I took ecstasy was indescribably wonderful. Drac and I had been mooching around town on a Wednesday night when we bumped into Rob Wood's younger brother, Giles, who had a couple of 'clear caps' for sale. 'Clear Caps', 'White Doves', 'Red and Blacks'..... I couldn't help noticing that the counterculture was just as obsessed with branding as the capitalist bastards they claimed to oppose. That said, I suppose you had to call them something.

Back at the ranch, we swallowed the capsules of fine white powder and waited. I happened to come up first. It was the cleanest, most ethereal ascension to a shimmering state of mildly psychedelic euphoria that I could ever have imagined. When Drac 'arrived' 20 minutes later, it became a heavenly union of like minded souls. The trouble was that I was never quite able to replicate the experience. I'd go as far as to say that every subsequent pill over the next several years was incrementally less fantastic.

Perhaps that's why confirmed 'e - heads' were in the habit of taking multiple pills in one sitting but, for some reason, I was wary of going down that road. Looking back, it's a shame I couldn't apply the same caution to every other drug of my habitual acquaintance.

Juggling the lower 6th harem parties with the illicit rave scene element, perhaps it was inevitable that we were headed for an intemperate explosion of some sort. By November, Rob Wood had moved into one of the spare rooms and immediately threatened the dynamic of the Utopia we were trying to build. Still labouring under the misapprehension that we quite liked him, Drac and I had welcomed our old school associate with open arms when he let it be known that the parental regime at Langtoft Road was cramping his style. Within a week of the new arrangement, it seemed inconceivable we had ever held him in even middling regard.

He was simply intolerable, forever banging on about 'mental evolution', 'love cabbages', 'dream machines' and obscure drugs that probably didn't exist. He wasn't even paying rent since such a 'bread-headed' agenda had never occurred to us. Nevertheless, the whole butterfly effect of his regrettable presence would soon have a profound impact on my future.

On Friday November 29, 1991 things went too far. We'd been pushing our luck in previous weeks as the parties got bigger and bigger, thanks to the addition of decks, P.A systems and appearances from allegedly popular local DJs who brought an altogether different faction to the 16 year old girls and old school mates. Suddenly the house was awash with drug dealers, free party people, high maintenance coke whores and fashion victim rave kids with VICKS inhalers hanging from their necks.

The police had been called a few times and one particular Sergeant had been keen to stress that it was in our best interests to keep the noise down since he had no desire for his officers to enter the premises and make copious arrests under the Misuse of Drugs

Act. But on this occasion, as Friday converged into Saturday, it was beyond obvious that we were caught in the cross fire of a full blown illegal rave, plunging the rural town into a state of unbridled chaos.

Police road blocks attempted to bar the way of raver convoys heading into the valley from as far out as Bristol, Bath and beyond. Many abandoned their cars and followed the beat, eventually trampling though the back gardens of Marling Crescent homeowners to their common destination. It was a monument to the concept of attraction over promotion although word was allegedly being circulated over pirate radio stations.

Every room of the house was as densely populated as a rush hour Central Line train and hordes congregated outside as the more enterprising collectives set up trade stands, selling water and ecstasy. A group of alleged 'gangstas' from Gloucester even had the temerity to request an admission fee from any new arrivals sufficiently gullible to drop an arbitrary fee into their plastic buckets. In a few days time, Chief Inspector Eddie Baud would be quoted in the Gloucester Citizen declaring, "At one point, in the early hours of Saturday morning there were several hundred people in the area."

I had taken a pill and felt agreeably fragile, sitting on the floor of what had been my bedroom as a teenager. With reference to the abject mayhem that engulfed us, Drac said, "This is the last night, I reckon. Good one to go out on." Suddenly we heard screams as scores of people came thundering down the staircase as if the house was under siege by urban guerrillas. Despite the delicate state that both of us were in, it clearly warranted investigation.

We jostled past random revellers, still seeking to flee the scene, and headed upstairs towards the dining room at the back of the house.
Upon arrival, I saw a stocky man with short blonde hair maniacally smashing the French Windows with a large spade whilst shouting, "I'M WARNING YOU… I'M ONE EVIL BASTARD….!"

The glass shattered and sprinkled in a most attractive way, almost as if I was watching a cartoon and this wasn't really happening at all. Confused rather than scared or annoyed, I asked what the devil was his problem but before he could answer, the sound of sirens permeated the air, causing our impromptu vandal to flee back over the fence into what I assumed was his own garden. Already plotting revenge, I told Drac to make a note of the house number. Although we didn't realise at the time, he had merely been complaining about the noise.

Downstairs, on the driveway there was a standoff with the local constabulary on one side of the fence and the rave contingent on the other. As I approached for the purpose of negotiation, I noticed that one of the special police constables was a lad I went to school with by the name of Shaun Scott. He had a beard and already looked about 40. 'What a wanker,' I was forced to conclude. I explained to the officer in charge that the situation had spiralled out of my control and I had little choice but to wait for people to leave of their own free will in the next several hours. It was the truth and there was nothing they could so about it, short of inducing a full scale riot. The Boys (and Girls) In Blue retreated but continued to observe the proceedings from the top of Little Mill Farm.

Indoors, the party was back in full swing and people were still arriving, despite the strategic police blockades and the surrounding devastation of broken windows, graffiti daubed walls and copious debris. Girls danced on speakers like podium starlets in a hip London night club whilst shady characters unknown to me peddled their various chemical wares. We had fucked up royally this time and Mum was going to disown me. And for what...? I didn't even like these people or the God awful cacophony they called 'music.'

At 2pm on Saturday November 30, as the last of the pie eyed stragglers were leaving, environmental health officer Derek Ind triumphantly served me with a noise abatement order under the 1990 Noise Pollution Act. He was accompanied by a terribly nice copper who assured me, "Ben, I'm on your side but this place is a fucking den, mate."

I made him right. Whatever grand designs I'd had at the outset, I sure as hell hadn't wanted any of this.

7/ HEROIN

She walked topless across the landing, her arms folded across her breasts for modesty's sake. She was elfin, blue eyed, button nosed and auburn haired. Rob must have got lucky last night, I thought. Superfluously, she apologised for her state of undress with appropriate shyness.

"Sorry….! Hi…Emma….
I saw you at the party. Ben isn't it…?"

She retrieved a burgundy and black top from the sofa and put it on with her back to me. Emma had met Rob last night at 'Grays', the local night club, and elected to come back with him. She'd been at the party last week it transpired and casual fate had brought her back through these hallowed portals. She sat down and we chatted for a few minutes until Rob entered the lounge, seating himself beside her on the couch as he began to roll a spliff, his sheepdog mop of dark hair obscuring his face.

"Are there any edibles about…?" he enquired. Everything about him was irksome. All victuals were 'edibles', cigarettes and weed were 'smokeables' and acid, cocaine and ecstasy were 'Class As. If a person happened to be in possession of any of the above, they would inevitably be asked to '2's up.' But I can never recall the generosity being returned on the rare occasions when he had something to offer. I told him there was no food on the premises but hastened to add that various convenience stores within acceptable proximity would be perfectly happy to sell him some at competitive rates. Emma seemed like a nice girl and one could only hope that whatever slender charm he had exercised upon her would wear off in due course.

After showering and picking out some appropriate regalia, I took the half hour walk into town, having arranged to meet Drac in the Pelican. Things had gone downhill of late and he had pretty much moved back to his Mum's. It had been a week since the party to end all parties, my mother was officially not speaking to me and steps were being taken to evict us. The dream was turning sour.

4 months on, I had written a couple of good songs but made no

progress in putting a band together. The plan had been for Drac to learn bass to a passable standard - perhaps marginally better than Sid Vicious - but it just wasn't happening. He seemed to think he had already commandeered the essential trappings of a rock star lifestyle: Beautiful young alternative girlfriend, the sexual freedom of an open relationship and an unrelenting blizzard of illicit pharmaceutical delights. With such things in place, what was the point in fucking about with tabs and scales...? The difference was that I was in it for the music as well as the debauchery. Or so I liked to think.

Since the American excursion, I had been climbing a chemical ladder that could be charted in reasonable order:

Marijuana - Check
Cocaine - Check
LSD - Check
Ecstasy - Check
Ketamine (not recommended) - Check
Speed - Check
Magic Mushrooms - Check

For the vast majority of Stroud's bright young bohemians, heroin was a step too far. It was the cut off point and 'not cool, maaaan.' The generation that had gleefully rejected the vacuous lies of 'Just Say No' still appeared to believe the public service announcements of the mid 80s in which young girls were warned that 'smack' might lead to acne and eventually languishing in a dark alleyway with the once popular kid who now resembled Freddy Kruger. I couldn't get my head around the hypocrisy.

In stark contrast to the media stereotype, there seemed to be a code of ethics amongst the truly condemned junkies not to sell to fresh faced newbies like myself and Drac. Ask them if they knew where you could score a bit of 'brown' and one would think you had casually enquired about a recent child murder. 'Leave it alone...' they said. 'Wish I'd never done it," they would add. This, of course, made us all the more determined to overcome their reluctance. Blade himself had imbued in me a fascination; such was the strange hybrid of reverence and disgust that he harboured for the notorious poppy derivative.

He confessed to having had 'a bit of a problem' in the immediate post punk days of the early 80s but described the heavenly high as 'a warm blanket over all your problems.' Then he would speak of the dire consequences resulting from predictable over indulgence and the wretched pond life that embodied the scene. His inconclusive musings on the whole topic left me unsure if I should dive headlong into a vat of opiates or reach for the garlic and rosary beads.

After careful consideration, I plumped for the first option. Drac and I were on a mission today and would not be denied. I entered the 'Pelly' via the main doors and saw him seated in the pit where the pool table resided nursing a Southern Comfort and lemonade. I ordered a pint of Directors from 'Beaver' the barman before joining my friend on the lower deck in order to discuss tactics.

It so happened that Drac's elder brother was a heroin addict and an 'eminent' one at that. When you went to Stroud General Hospital claiming to have a smack habit, they would initially put you on a methadone 'script' that was picked up every week. After a period of assessment, some of the deemed hopeless cases would he upgraded to ampoules of diamorphine, dispensed daily from Boots pharmacy, excepting Sundays. Phil was one of those incorrigibles in receipt of the much sought after 'amps.' But Drac had a better chance of winning the Miss Black America pageant than scoring from him directly.

Far from standing us in good stead, the association worked to our detriment as most of the junkies knew he was Phil's little brother and, consequently, wouldn't touch either one of us with a barge pole. Nonetheless, when you're dealing with addicts, you will always find somebody who is willing to compromise. In this instance, that somebody came in the shape of Willem. A ludicrously good looking bastard with more charm than a Mayfair finishing school, Willem was a contemporary of Phil's and a gear head himself, although he didn't fit the stereotype. He reckoned he could help us out but "Not until 7 O' Clock.."

The Pelican was the kind of local in which you could sit on a drink for hours without fear of harassment from the bar staff, so we played the waiting game, amusing ourselves with intermittent games of pool and the usual passionate conversations about art and music. I'd been drinking like a fish in the States but the recent interest in all things narcotic had certainly checked my burgeoning alcoholism. Booze was still desirable but drugs were the fiscal priority.

At around 7.30pm, Willem returned as promised and motioned for us to come to the back of the pub near the garden entrance. 'The Man' was nearby he explained and it would cost us £12.50, "Unless you wanna' go for the full £25..?" Deciding on the cheaper option. I handed him the cash and he sloped off in the direction of Iceland on Kendrick Street, pledging to return forthwith. Less than 5 minutes later he was back, handing me a tightly packed rizla paper sealed in cellophane. Transcending the seemingly Masonic barrier and scoring our first wrap of smack was all well and good but how were we supposed to take it...? After briefly attempting to demonstrate the technique required for 'chasing the dragon', our facilitator shrugged, "Actually, I'd snort it if I were you. If you 'cook' it you'll probably lose half of it.."

We headed back to Brooklands in Drac's Triumph Acclaim and, mercifully, the house was empty when we arrived. The last thing we needed was Rob's ambience on the night of such a crucial experiment. Despite Willem's advice, we didn't fancy snorting the gear. Jim Morrison was rumoured to have died snorting heroin, having thought it was cocaine, back in 1971. Being, himself, one of our main posthumous gurus, it wasn't a precedent we were inclined to ignore.

Consequently, we cut the top off a plastic bottle, with the intention of placing it over the silver foil and sucking up the fumes through the makeshift funnel. As I put on a Velvet Underground CD, Drac carefully opened the rizla paper and examined the contents. "It's a tiny amount," he announced suspiciously. Willem had probably nipped us to some degree but it was impossible to gauge since neither one of us had any idea what 12 and a half quid's worth of heroin ought to look like.

Drac sprinkled a little of the brown powder onto a square of tin foil as I hovered over it with the bottle top pressed to my lips. He held a lighter flame underneath which instantly turned the powder into molten brown lava giving off toxic vapours that I inhaled and held inside for a long as I could. 30 seconds later, I exhaled a thick stream of smoke and felt an instant warm flushing of the skin. My eyes seemed to roll back in my head as I croaked, "It comes on quick."

I swapped the bottle top for the lighter and foil in order to facilitate the same process for him. As he exhaled, I could see his pupils had constricted quite radically. In junky parlance, it was known as being 'pinned.' We went back and forth a few times until Drac suddenly felt nauseous and began to vomit into a white polythene bag that was lying around. Everyone had told me that throwing up was inevitable the first time. Even the TV adverts had explained that much. But, actually, I didn't feel like being sick.

It was vaguely pleasant but hardly the mind blowing, other worldly high of popular underground folklore. And Drac spewing up into a plastic bag did nothing to enhance the experience. We lay on the living room floor, hoping that horizontal silence would lead to an astral voyage but I just felt comfortably numb and soon fell asleep. A few days later, Jenny would ask Drac what it had been like. "It was crap," he would reply. I wasn't inclined to be quite so negative but struggled to imagine that the drug would ever exert any kind of hold over me.

On January 17, 1992, we decided to get even with 'Mr. Spade.' It had been 7 weeks since that idiot had decimated the French windows and he couldn't be allowed to get away with it. Up to now, we had tossed the odd sack of refuse over his garden fence that was duly thrown back upon discovery but it wasn't nearly enough redress for the damage he had done. We hadn't even had the glass replaced which left the house totally unprotected except by continual occupancy. It seems ludicrous looking back but home security and personal safety were clearly not amongst our priorities.

After sharing a bottle of Southern Comfort on the night in question, I put it to Drac that Muhammad Ali's 50th birthday should be commemorated in some fitting way. "How about we get a brick and put it through that cunt's window...?" he suggested. I agreed that retribution was long overdue. Great believers in the decree of chance, we tossed a coin to ascertain which of us should do the deed. It fell on me. I put on my leather jacket and hurried down the stairs while my resolve was at a premium.

Marling Crescent was but 5 minutes walk away and I was soon stood outside No.17 at around half past midnight, holding an appropriately sized rock sourced from Little Mill Farm. The cul de sac was deathly quiet as if suburbia had gone to bed in its entirety. But would somebody hear the smashing of glass...? Reluctant to trespass, I stood by the gate and hurled the stone at the kitchen window. It bounced harmlessly off the sill and I sprinted back in the direction of home base, feeling less than heroic.

"Maybe we're not supposed to do this...?" pondered Drac when informed of my innocuous failure. At the time, we set plenty of store by the concept of fatalism. Still brave from Janis Joplin's favourite liqueur, he immediately reconsidered. "Bollocks, I'm gonna' do it..!" He plucked his long black coat from the banister and strode downstairs with a greater sense of purpose than I had exhibited. With a sense of understatement lifted from Hollywood movies, he declared, "I'll be back."

When he returned 10 minutes later, he bore a look of triumphal satisfaction, befitting a man who had achieved so much more than simply smashing someone's kitchen window. I sought confirmation. He nodded. "Missed the first time and ended walking right up to the window and putting it straight through. Smoked a fag in his garden, too." If that was true, then it was clear that neither the occupants of No.17 nor the neighbours had been disturbed by the noise. Mission accomplished, we were ready to hit the hay, or the floor and the sofa in our respective sleeping bags. Lately, we had forsaken the bedrooms for no particular reason. As I drifted into a heavy sleep, the extreme likelihood of reprisals couldn't have been further from my mind.

I was harshly awoken the next morning by a sharp bang on the head. It was all happening very quickly but I could see Mr. Spade standing over me, brandishing what looked like a cricket bat handle and screaming, "WHAT ARE YOU DOING TO US…?!!" It seemed a strangely ineffectual weapon but I had no time to think about that. I scrambled to my feet and grabbed him by the scuff of the neck with my left hand then threw a straight right that landed on his cheekbone causing a cut. I followed the momentum of the punch and wrestled him to the ground. Having dropped the cricket bat handle, he suddenly picked up the empty Southern Comfort bottle that lay on the floor and attempted to get some leverage from his awkward position. He feebly swatted at my thigh in token defiance as I called for backup.

"DRAC, HELP ME… HE'S GOT A BOTTLE.."

Apparently oblivious to the proceedings, Drac irritably rubbed his eyes, demanding to know, "WHO'S got a bottle…?"

Having processed the basic tenets of the situation, he sidled out of the sleeping bag and approached our grappling forms. Reaching down, he gently took the bottle from Mr. Spade's right hand and placed it on the mantelpiece above the fireplace. Having fulfilled that pressing obligation, he climbed straight back into 'bed' and closed his eyes. It might sound implausible but that's what he did.

Disarmed and now horizontal on the hard floor with both arms behind his back, Mr. Spade suddenly asked, "WHY CAN'T WE

TALK ABOUT THIS…?" His sudden interest in non violent arbitration seemed borderline hysterical but I wasn't the spiteful type and neither was Drac. I allowed him to regain his feet and instructed him to follow me through the long since empty window frames and into what passed for our back garden. (It was the same way he had gained entry, of course.) "Ok, I'm listening," I told him.

"If you're gonna' be staying here then we're gonna' have to sort this out, aren't we..?" he reasoned in a voice that seemed at least half an octave higher all of a sudden.

"We call it quits now and you're getting off lightly," I said. He nodded.

"You stay out of my way and I'll stay out of your way," he said. I nodded. He walked away, noticeably taking the long route home instead of climbing back over the fence. Perhaps it was a mark of respect. I stepped back into the lounge to find Drac fully awake and in good humour. On the floor in 3 separate pieces were the fragments of a child's cricket bat. Suddenly it made sense why he had appeared to be attacking me with its mere handle when I awoke. I could only assume it had broken on my head after the first strike.

That we could regard the scene that had just unfolded as a relatively normal start to the weekend was probably worrying in itself but I had a far more urgent concern that I duly voiced:

"I don't know about you but I could murder a bit of breakfast…."

8/ EXODUS

By February, I was sharing the house with an unwanted gaggle of uncharismatic wastrels. Marianne, who resembled a less aesthetically pleasing version of the Tank Girl caricature and seemed to think the world owed her a living. Bernie the Traveller, whom I'd allowed to park a trailer on the drive along with his herd of wild goats. Wayne, a good looking recently straight kid who had undergone a Grange Hill level of exaggerated decline after smoking his first joint a few months ago.

Aside from such stand outs there was an assorted shower of pseudo bohemian wankers in dungarees who smoked endless dope to a mind numbing sound track of sub trance/ elevator bollocks. How had it come to this...? These crusty, 17th generation hippies had nothing in common with any youthful, rebellious impulse I had ever felt. And the whole left wing/ anti - capitalist stance was a crock of shit, too. Most of them were as grasping and self interested as the next person in any remotely real life situation. Down the line, they would either be drug dependent pan handlers or reformed insurance brokers. It was that simple.

On the plus side, Rob had moved out and Emma had moved in. As expected, she had quickly grown weary of his grating personality and briefly defected to his brother, Giles, which had resulted in a violent skirmish between the two siblings. The Giles fling burned out within a couple of weeks and soon we were free to explore the chemistry that she and I undoubtedly had. I'd gone as far as taking her to London for a weekend and introducing her to Blade who was now living in Ham. We stayed at Mt. Ararat Road but nothing physical happened. I really wasn't good at making the first move.

One night in the last days of the Brooklands chapter, we each took a trip and finally succumbed to our feelings before expressing them carnally as the sun rose. Thereafter, we morphed into an inseparable couple almost instantly. An inseparable couple who needed to find a new place to live as it happened. The legal eviction process had gotten as far as a week's notice to quit the premises. Ignoring all predictable pleas from the useless and self interested to 'stand and fight', I informed my assemblage of sedentary dossers that they had 3 days to leave the building. They didn't like it but none of them were going to argue with me. Despite my appearance, I had a reputation for being able to handle myself and the broken cricket bat story had already passed into local legend.

As soon as I was satisfied that the house was expunged of freeloaders, Emma and I spent a few days at her parents' place in Eastcombe before hitching to London in search of new horizons. Arriving at our destination, we slept on Dad's floor for a few nights before finding a room above a restaurant on Petersham Road for £80 a week. It was a lot of money in 1992 for a bedroom in which we were not allowed to entertain guests but this was Richmond when all said and done.

Emma wasn't a bad singer, although not lead vocalist material, which suited me fine. Actually, I couldn't abide a girl with a big ballsy rock voice. Women (in context of music) should provide sweet, lilting harmonies for my twisted perfect pop songs, I fancied. In truth, I had only written 4 vaguely decent songs at this point but listen to me wax lyrical about my impending greatness and you would think I already had David Bowie's back catalogue under my belt. I had classic delusions of grandeur but try telling me and I'd punch you in the face.

Emma got a job in a betting shop opposite Richmond Market because somebody had to and it wasn't going to be me. I genuinely believed I was an investment and would provide our ascension to fame and fortune soon enough. 'Just stick with me, baby...' was the essential bullet point. In addition to my reluctance to a get a job, I was a jealous god and a cultural Nazi. I made it uncomfortable for anyone in my circle to express even moderate approval for any music, literature or comedy that didn't fall within my decidedly narrow parameters of acceptable taste. Looking back, I must have been a veritable joy.

Before long, in order to supplement her income, we decided to take the plunge and try a bit of busking on the District Line.

For years, I had seen musicians of variable merit serenading commuters on the tube, from winos with penny whistles to the genuinely talented and tragically undiscovered. I had sung to mostly drunk live audiences in Colorado but had yet to sing and play guitar at once in any public setting. Beneath the bravado, I wasn't sure if I was good enough but the addition of a pretty girl who could carry a tune seemed unlikely to do me any harm.

Entering the carriage at the rear end of the train at Richmond, I made a brief introduction to the assembled passengers before launching into an Andy Blade number called 'The Amazing Adventures.' You need projection and balance to make a go of performing on a moving underground train full of people who instinctively seek to ignore you. Considering we were virgins in this regard, our opening rendition seemed quite well received. There was a smattering of applause and when Emma walked up and down the aisle with a black velvet bag, enough people dropped in coins to make the enterprise appear credible.

Buoyed by this initial success, we spent the next 2 hours playing the same song between Richmond and Earls Court and back again. Inevitably, there were objections from a few disgruntled members of the public who took exception at being forced to endure something that they didn't ask for but I had a quiver full of ripostes and relished the conflict. We had amassed over £25 when we chose to call it a night and return to our bolt hole on Richmond Hill.

It should have been all the confidence I needed to get busy during Emma's working hours and put some food on the table but I was reluctant to go without her and fate was about to whisk us in another direction. A few days later, she returned home in the afternoon laden with shopping bags containing garments for both of us, bottles of Southern Comfort and a surfeit of appropriately selected CDs. Her mischievous grin spoke for itself. She had abused her Barclays cheque book, spending money she didn't have on a therapeutic splurge of consumerism. Excellent, I thought. The worst we could expect was a curt letter from the bank in which

some nameless account manager would confess to being 'extremely disappointed.'
And we would be gone before it hit the doormat.

"Let's go to France," she said with spontaneous vigour. Making her case, she pointed out that we had no social scene In Richmond outside of Blade and she was tired of working behind a kiosk getting propositioned by luckless, lecherous twats. Most of her money was consumed by the rent and it seemed like a fine time to give our notice in favour of a continental sojourn. I made her right. Our London experience had been rather lame hitherto and if we could earn money on London Transport with our dulcet tones then there seemed no reason why we couldn't do the same in Paris and various other European cities. Although I was supposed to be the leader there was no point in quibbling over a good idea.

We gave a week's notice to the old Italian spinster who owned the house and made our travel arrangements. 7 days later, leaving any surplus belongings at Dad's for safekeeping, we caught a train to Dover and then hopped on a late ferry to Calais, checking in at the first cheap hotel we could find. The following morning after breakfast, we took the train to Paris. The journey took almost 3 hours and it was early evening when we arrived at Gare Du Nord with 2 rucksacks and an acoustic guitar. Boarding the metro, we plotted a course to the 3 Ducks Hostel in the 15th arrondissement near Rue Du Commerce.

The 3 Ducks was billed as 'the oldest private hostel in France' and had a wild party reputation. In 7 years time it would assume a major significance in my ragged story but, on this occasion, we kept to ourselves and checked into a double room on the second floor of the former 18th century coaching house. I was too possessive and guarded to hang out with the assorted international backpackers whilst having my woman in tow and so we went out to dinner instead.

Disembarking at a random stop in another part of the city, we walked for a while and drank in the exquisite scenes of nocturnal Paris. The lights and glowing yellow headlamps. The innumerable pharmacies, vibrant cafe terraces and strikingly chic pedestrians. It ought to have been romantic but I was already concerned about money. We would need to start busking immediately just to stay afloat. Suddenly it began to rain hard causing us to seek refuge in a nearby Bistro that looked lively and affordable. Duly seated at a table we ordered a pizza for 2 billed as the 'Romeo et Juliet' and the cheapest bottle of house red. The bill would almost clean us out but tomorrow was another day.

Back on the street and subject to a degree of geographical confusion, I asked two passing gentlemen of Latin appearance for directions to the nearest Metro station. Both appeared to be in their 20s but only one of them was conversant in our mother tongue.

"You are English..? You come with us, I show you..."

As we continued down the street, our new friend introduced himself as Julio. His non bi lingual sidekick went by the name of Victor. "We are not French," he was keen to stress, "We are Portuguese." Before we reached the Metro, he asked, "Would you like to come for a beer...?"

I told him we were a little financially embarrassed to which he replied, "If I invite you for a beer, I pay..." Not wishing to seem ungrateful, we duly repaired to a nearby bar and our host ordered 3 lagers and a glass of white wine for Emma. Julio said it was important that we remain standing as many Parisian bars would charge double for a drink if you sat on the terrace. We told a little of our back-story. The plans for busking in the short term and our desire to form a band that would parlay us into stardom.

"I have 3 guitars," announced Julio enthusiastically.

"What kind of music do you play...?" Emma wondered.

"Things I love," came the response.

He ordered another round of drinks before saying." If you would like…after tomorrow, you don't stay at the hostel, you stay with me. I have bunk beds, I hope is ok…?"

The decision to accept was ultimately mine but we both instinctively trusted him despite the brevity of our acquaintance. And given our impoverished circumstances, we were scarcely in a position to refuse. With free bed and board, we could hope to save most of the busking revenue in order to finance the next leg of our jaunt to Amsterdam, Barcelona or Madrid. Assuming there would be any busking revenue to begin with, of course. The future was uncertain but here I was again, landing squarely on my feet in a foreign city, it seemed. In fairness to Emma, I couldn't claim all the credit for our serendipity on this occasion.

"Meet me in this bar tomorrow at 5 O' Clock," instructed Julio. Thanking him in unison profusely, we made our way to the Metro station on the corner and headed back to Felix Faure on Line 8. Faithful to Lonely Planet reviews, the party was in session at Chez 3 Ducks but I insisted we swerve the glass clinking revelry in the courtyard and retire to bed.

I wasn't single and neither was I ready to mingle.

9/ AMSTERDAMNED

The next morning we rose early and took advantage of the free breakfast offered by the hostel, consisting of baguettes, orange juice and coffee. Conveniently, they also had a luggage room, typically for check outs who didn't want to spend their last day in the French Capital laden with heavy baggage. After showering in a space that would have made a telephone box seem cavernous, we dumped our rucksacks and headed out with the guitar and a plastic cup for the acceptance of coinage. Boarding the train at Commerce, I made my threadbare introduction: "Bonjour Madames and Monsieurs...Un Chanson Pour Vous..." If banter was half the battle in London then it was now all about the music:

'THE AMAZING ADVENTURES OF FRANK HOBLIN
AMAZING ADVENTURES OF FRANK HOBLIN
HE LIVES IN A WORLD WHERE YOU CAN'T GO
IN A MYSTICAL LAND
WHERE THE FLOWERS GROW....'

The opening salvo was not met with thunderous applause but Emma collected about 15 francs which presumably meant we weren't going to starve. I thanked the captive crowd with due haste as we scurried onto the next carriage and repeated the process. Feeling more anonymous in a foreign setting we began to expand our 1 song repertoire, juggling more Andy Blade numbers with Beatles and Stones covers plus the odd Morrissey tune. 'Mozzer' was allegedly quite popular in these parts as the audible fanfare on 'Beethoven Was Deaf' would later attest.

The first rule of underground busking can be written in stone: When you find a song that seems to loosen the public purse, you tear the arse out of it until you literally can't sing the words anymore. The first song is called the 'A side.' The second song, played as a gratis after the money has been collected, is known as the 'B side.' At this point, the pressure is off and you can play whatever you damn well please. An A side should be loud and upbeat. A poignant, arpeggiated ballad will go down like a lead balloon, without amplification. These were the basic tenets we would quickly learn on the road.

Working the route from Commerce to Concorde for several hours, we stopped for a bite to eat near the Eiffel Tower and counted the spoils. Although levels of public appreciation and disapproval were more subdued than at home, the earnings seemed roughly equivalent. We had nearly 400 francs which constituted a fair day's work after expenses. Back at the 3 Ducks, we swapped the deluge of coins for notes at the bar and retrieved our bags before heading off to meet Julio.

He was as good as his word, arriving on the dot of 5pm at the bar with his cheerfully mute companion. He ordered a round of drinks and asked, "For how long do you want to stay…?"

"2 to 3 weeks if it's not too much trouble…?" I suggested.

"Ok.." he nodded.

We finished our drinks and caught the Metro to Exelmans in the 16th. Julio and Victor lived in a large tenement block on Rue du Général Delestraint with a blizzard of relatives who were hard to keep track of in their entirety. The heads of the household were Julio's elder sister, Claudia, and her fiancé, Maxim, who resembled an Italian matinee idol. They were lovely, unpretentious people who treated us as their own for the next 3 weeks. Besides Julio, only Claudia spoke English. Introductions having been made, we congregated in the large kitchen that doubled up as the dining room and communal area, drinking wine and Pastis by the bucket load. Guitars were produced and a jam session ensued as some of the younger female cousins giggled and whispered amongst themselves about the strangely dressed English couple who were suddenly the centre of attention.

That night, we took the bottom bunk in Julio's room whilst he slept above. I got the feeling we were ousting Victor but had no idea where he might have gone as a contingency. Julio worked on a construction site somewhere in the city and was up early every morning on that account. He gave us a key to the main building with the sole proviso that we must "Never bring Arabian people here…" A strange edict but not one we were likely to disobey.

The ensuing days were a blur of busking, boozy communal meal times and Sunday afternoon games of football in Bois de Boulonge. Julio would probably have been happy to extend his hospitality a little longer but a deal was a deal. In 3 weeks we had saved enough to take a train to Amsterdam and try our luck in Europe's premier 'City of Sin.' Doing the rounds on the Metro, we had met an old American busker called Val who said there were rich pickings to be had in Rembrandtpleine and Leidsepleine Square. "Playing is no problem but you've got a lot of competition," he warned. I hated competition but hid my insecurities behind a sneering contempt for other street musicians who just 'didn't get it.'

On the last day in Paris, Emma and I had a tiff leading to mutual threats that our union was over. We ignored each other for a couple of hours but had predictably resolved our differences by nightfall as we boarded a train from Gare Du Nord at a half past midnight. Snatching a bit of sleep in transit, we arrived at Amsterdam Centraal Station at 6am and jumped on a tram to the 'Sleep Inn' hostel. It was unclear where one could purchase tram tickets and nobody seemed to care if passengers paid or not. Unattended bicycles were also fair game, we would later be told. It was too early to check in at the cheapest crash pad in town but we paid for our reservations and left our bags in the storage room before taking a stroll around the city.

Amsterdam is a well documented smoker's paradise but I hated hash and weed by now. I just wasn't getting the wonderful buzz that others seemed to extract from cannabis. It made me feel queasy, disoriented and self conscious. Furthermore, lifestyle devotees of the drug generally had dire taste in music and woeful dress sense. A hard drugs habit might be sordidly glamorous but marijuana worship was simply lame, I thought.

After a bit of breakfast and a soft drink at 'The Doors' coffee shop, I suggested we go in search of Rembrandtplein, which turned out to be a 15 minute tram ride away. By 9.30 am, the numerous cafe terraces were filling up with tourists as a horde of international buskers waited in line. Val wasn't lying about competition. Every day would see a surfeit of performers from all over the world, seeking to charm the ever revolving audience. The majority were guitarists and singers but trumpet players, violinists, acrobats, jugglers and street clowns also vied for attention.

There was a rotational system in place that everyone in this clique abided by. Each act got to play the designated terrace for 20 minutes after which it was agreed that the next act would wait 20 minutes before starting their performance thus giving the crowd a chance to mutate. There were about 8 terraces in the square and the stalwarts would play between 10 to 15 sets a day. To survive in this ecosystem we would have to up our game. It was no longer a one song hit and run gig. On the first day we played whatever we had in our locker - 'Amazing Adventures', 'Girl', 'Norwegian Wood', 'Wild Horses', 'Working Class Hero', 'Ask.' Having hit the 100 Guilder mark by mid afternoon, we opted to call it quits and explore our new surroundings.

Aesthetically, it was a beautiful city with its canals, parks, museums and gabled architecture. Nonetheless, it was impossible to denude the overriding context of cheap vice; Drugs, commercial prostitution, Brits on the piss and Haight - Ashbury rejects languishing in an omnipresent fog of THC. Walking through Dam Square, Emma got talking to an English girl from up North who was earning a crust from the evidently popular craze of 'hair wrapping.' Her name was Stella.

"Do you know of any places going..?" asked Emma.

"Actually, the people at the house I live in are looking to rent the room next to mine for 25 Guilders a day. I can give you the address if you wanna' go and see it..?"

She borrowed a pen from a passing tourist and scrawled the address on a scrap of paper. The house was on Derde Oosterparkstaat, wherever that might be. "You can catch the 51 to Wibustraat and it's a 10 minute walk," advised Stella. "Nobody pays," she added, confirming our first impressions.

Jackie and Mel were an English couple in their 30s and represented themselves as the owners of what might have been a squat. Jackie was on the gear and bore the trademarks of premature ravaging. Mel was a balding, wispy haired yokel from Dursley of all places. Upon hearing of our mutual West Country heritage, he claimed to have once gotten the better of Stroud legend, Danny Gardiner, in a prison altercation. Perhaps he was setting out his stall early doors in case I got any big ideas about the household pecking order. It wasn't The Ritz but the room next to Stella's was spacious at least and conveniently adjoined the kitchen. The deal was simple: 25 Guilders a day except for Sundays which were given as a 'freebie.' For the equivalent of £66 a week, it seemed a fair deal. After perusing the bathroom facilities and conferring with Emma, I handed Mel 25 Guilders and shook on the deal. The management of the 'Sleep Inn' were surprisingly happy to refund our money and so we moved in that same evening.

After a couple of weeks finding our feet on Rembrandtplein, we joined forces with a Russian lead guitarist called Herman. A tall, good looking guy with slightly thinning blonde hair and the hint of a tan, Herman had come to the Dutch capital whilst touring with a Russian folk band and opted to abscond. Only recently liberated from what he called 'the pressure of the communists' he was obsessed with gadgets and couldn't seem to get his head around the opulence of an 'All You Can Eat' pizza deal.

It was at this point that we truly morphed into the Andy Blade Tribute Band, playing such late 80s nuggets as 'Church Bell', 'Creature' and '3 Weeks' - inviting the natural assumption they were self penned. Herman's amplified licks and musical arrangements greatly lifted the songs and Emma was coming into her own on backing vocals. Objectively, I could say that we had a credible act by now and bigger plans besides daily subsistence on the streets of Amsterdam.

The king of buskers on Rembrandtplein was Juro - a street clown and slapstick comedy genius with balls of steel. He had a vaguely Eskimo appearance and wore a long beige Mac and beret as he set about creating ad hoc theatre through the medium of mischief. His commitment to the show would occasionally solicit attacks from angry members of the public who didn't see the funny side of having their hat stolen or their girlfriend's trousers marginally yanked down from behind. It was an occupational hazard but the tram drivers all played along as he clambered across their windscreens proffering cones of chips or ice creams snatched from unsuspecting bystanders.

When Juro performed he played to the entire square and brought it to a standstill once a day, 5 days a week. His earnings might have required a Securicor van to transport the monies back to the luxurious squat he reportedly shared with his beautiful actress wife. He was one cool motherfucker and no mistake.

All things considered it should have been the time of my life. Young, in love, footloose and fancy free. But I was a tortured soul, constantly haranguing myself for the abject failure to become a prolific song writing genius. I was so desperate to record my life that I seemed incapable of living it organically and found it impossible to enjoy any music outside of the holy grail of bands that I worshipped. And poor Emma was being dragged along in my sidecar.

By mid July, Mel had decided he could make more money out of the place if he turned it into a low rent hostel catering to the Eastern European market. He claimed that 'costs' had risen and that we were nice people thus it wouldn't seem right increasing our rent like some 'Rachmaninoff'. I assumed he was referring to the late Peter Rachman and not the legendary Russian composer but we took the hint. Herman's Dutch flat mate was away so we went to stay with him for a fortnight before taking a house share in the suburbs with a contingent of young Bengali males who behaved as if they had never seen a woman up close before.

I wasn't enjoying any of it anymore. Nothing is fun when you have to do it every day and most of my confederate musicians were jaded and cynical The final straw came when one of the inhabitants of the new house came on to Emma in the kitchen as she sought to make morning coffee. That night, I took an ecstasy tablet and sat in the living room alone watching charmless Dutch TV. Eschewing soft porn, I switched the channel to a black and white film set in London and resolved there and then that we were going home.

The next day, saying goodbye to nobody besides Herman, we packed our things and boarded a coach to Victoria, 16 hours away. Amsterdam could sink into the mud for all I cared.

10/ NAT WEST, BARCLAYS, MIDLANDS, LLOYDS

By the spring of '93, we were living in a house near Gloucester Park and fast acquiring a taste for heroin. I'd been ambivalent on the first occasion with Drac but, shortly after getting home, Emma and I had scored a couple of 'ten bags' from a Stroud connection and the buzz suddenly made sense. The pleasant nausea and surge of invulnerability giving way to an out of body serenity seemed more reliable then the erratic rushes of ecstasy or the sheer unpredictability of LSD. My consciousness had expanded as much as I wanted it to.

Our main envoys at the time were a couple of New Age Travellers called Chris and Tash. They were not dealers but addicts whom we inexplicably favoured as our brokers. Like most leftfield drug users they were utterly convinced that all phones were tapped by the Home Office and insisted on the use of a spurious code when communicating via landlines. "JUST SAY A NUMBER,.." Chris would bark in his Doncaster brogue. Accordingly, I would tell him how many bags we were after. If anyone actually had been listening in, it was hard to imagine these curt exchanges sounding anything besides blatantly conspiratorial.

Chris was an interesting and creative soul, albeit a little prone to romantic exaggeration. He had red brown matted dreadlocks, round specs and identified as a poet in the mould of John Cooper Clarke. Natasha was dark haired with olive skin and always seemed to be wearing a brown, fur trimmed 'aviator' jacket. Aside from taking heroin, she spent much of her time carving huge effigies of female genitalia into lumps of natural wood. Surprisingly, she would become moderately successful in later years, after getting clean. Perhaps the abstract art crowd could see themselves in her work.

Both were hopelessly obsessed with the junk lifestyle but predictably warned of its abyss. "Don't get a habit," cautioned Chris, "Just do it every Friday and you'll be ok." To his credit, he did rather limit the amounts of the evil drug that we were able to ingest. Frequently, they would be gone for several hours on the premise of some far flung mission to God knows where in pursuit of some 'top gear.' Eventually, they would roll up in their blue 1949 Ford Popular with the sealed bags and an appropriate tale of the outlandish circumstances that had been endured in their procurement. In hindsight, there seems little doubt that they were using our money to buy weighed amounts and robbing us blind on the deal. I can't say I blame them.

No.30 Weston Road was a 3 bed roomed property that we shared with a bloke called Anthony, who worked as assistant manager in the Cheltenham branch of H.Samuel, the jewellers. Originally from Leeds, he was an innocent if rather boring man who would be driven from the house before the year was out as a direct result of our shenanigans. He didn't deserve the harassment he would be subjected to but no doubt karma kept a note of the address.

Against the grain of this drug sponsored idleness, I decided to get a job for the summer. Quite what pointed me to a horticultural nursery in an outpost called Upper Leadon, I can't recall but the discreet mode of payment was probably a decisive factor. Every weekday morning at 7.30am, I would get a lift to work from a heavy metal fan and bass guitarist called Dave who lived on the other side of the park. Now 27, Dave had worked for Alan Bassett's Plant Nursery for several years but probably nursed dreams of 'making it' at some point. "My friends call me 'Monster'," he said on the first day. He wasn't a bad person by any stretch but I called him Dave throughout our brief acquaintanceship.

The job was pretty hard graft, abated twice a day by a mid morning break and half an hour for lunch. Nutrition was always welcome but conversation was thin on the ground. Aside from Dave, the entire workforce seemed to consist of local villagers, some of whom were inevitably related to each other. They had no life experience I could relate to and seemingly no aspirations beyond the endless transportation of hyacinths and chrysanthemums from one section of the greenhouse to another.

After 2 weeks of intellectual starvation, deliverance came in the form of a slightly built young man with catalogue model good looks and an Ambre Solaire complexion. Jon lived in nearby Tibberton and was only here because his father had insisted he get a job whilst living 'under our roof.' His eloquence and mental agility were readily apparent and we gravitated to one another immediately. We discussed music. He was into The Cure, exclusively it seemed and at the expense of all other bands. Clearly, he was going to need some education but I could live with that.

Curiously, Jon didn't eat anything at break times. When I remarked upon this departure from convention, he explained that he was too gut wrenchingly heartbroken to entertain the thought of digestion. In support of this claim he plucked a matchbox from his jeans pocket and opened it to reveal a passport sized photograph of a freckled blonde girl and a razor blade. The picture was of Gina, his love lost, and the razor blade had been retained as a last resort lest the pain of her capricious betrayal became too much to bear. It was either a bad photograph or he was flagrantly overreacting, I thought. Anyone would think he had gotten the elbow from Helen of Troy.

In retrospect, it seems obvious that Jon wasn't well but, far from recoiling at his intimate disclosure, I was happy to have met an interesting character in a cultural desert. I could relate to heartbreak and the threat of suicide. People wrote songs about such things. Nobody wrote about inbred yokels who worked in hothouses. Having found a kindred spirit, perhaps it was inevitable that we would soon concoct an exit plan.

The day shift finished at 4pm and so one Thursday afternoon I invited Jon back to Weston Road to meet Emma and my younger brother who was staying in the spare room for a few days. Barely 17, he had recently come out as gay and Mum was having a hard time with it. I suppose the liberal idealism that reigned in our household was a welcome antidote to any narrow mindedness he had encountered back in Chester.

After polite introductions over a cup of tea, it was decided we should head to Stroud in search of acid . Despite the adherence to heroin, I was still up for the odd psychedelic excursion in the right company. John said he had done it before but my brother, who shall retain his anonymity, certainly hadn't. In any case, I would soon learn that anything Jon said should be afforded the same credibility as a Sunday Sport expose about Martians living in the White House. It would take some unravelling but he had created an intricate back story that bore no resemblance to his actual life. At the time of our paths crossing, he represented himself as 20 years old, having been freshly kicked out of Oxford University in his second year for drug possession. Clearly, he imagined that such a bespoke 'resume' would impress me. I rated intelligence and so he had been to our greatest academic institution. But I was also a rebel and a non conformist hence he had thrown it all away due to being so dangerously subversive.

I would later discover that he was only 18 and had spent the last few months studying boat design at Falmouth Marine School before either leaving or getting expelled when he was nicked for shoplifting books on the Scilly Isles. But at this early stage of our friendship, as we boarded a train to Stroud, I had no reason to doubt his version of events. Perhaps be could be the bass player that Drac had failed to mature into. In all likelihood, he was more photogenic at least.

Arriving in Stroud, we scored 5 tabs in the graveyard from a character called 'Bent Nick', each swallowing one immediately before jumping on the next available service back to Gloucester. Starting to come up as we trudged back through the park towards Weston Road, a devilish plan began to form. We had one tab left over. Why not give it to Anthony in the name of sport...? Dosing a person against their volition with a radically mind altering substance like LSD is an extremely irresponsible, and even potentially tragic, thing to do. As the elder statesman of the group one might have hoped I would know better but history shows otherwise.

Back at the house, sipping tea and listening to 'The Smiths', we huddled in the front room, excitedly discussing the best way to 'spike' our unwitting housemate. After various ruses were suggested and rejected, it was finally decided to make a razor blade incision in a Malteser before inserting the tab into the tiny cavity thus created. Placing the loaded ball of chocolate back into box, we briefly pondered how he might be persuaded to eat the intended orb as opposed to one of its harmless counterparts. Then it came to me:

"Just tell the greedy fucker he can finish the whole lot…"

That settled it. Emma walked into the adjoining room that served as Anthony's lounge and offered him the surplus confectionery. He ought to have been suspicious but happily accepted the spheroid delights on which he began to nibble as he watched TV on the couch. Emma returned with a thumbs up. Now we simply had to play the waiting game. I kept an eye on Jon and my brother but both seemed to be handling it well. I suggested we go for a walk to the local shop, taking our mugs of tea with us in open defiance of conventional norms.

When we returned, loud rave style music could be heard emanating from Anthony's living room. I went to investigate and found him saucer eyed on the sofa, asking, "Do you like my new CD…? I think it sounds REALLY good….!" He had polished off the Maltesers and our rather dangerous practical joke appeared to have backfired. He was tripping out of his mind all right but clearly enjoying it. Grudgingly impressed, I left him to it.

As the night wore on, he played either the same compilation or something very similar until the small hours. Considering that he didn't know he was tripping and had to be up for work in the morning, his fluid adaptation to the situation was hilarious. "Perhaps he was just born to be a trip head," suggested Jon. Eventually, the anodyne noise concluded and, presumably, he fell asleep.

Jon and I called in sick the next day and never showed up for work again. In the weeks that followed, he moved into the spare room by degrees, spending less and less time at the house in Tibberton where his father and hated step mother lived. Although he had appreciated the impromptu trip, Anthony was less enamoured of various other juvenile pranks and opted to find alternative accommodation. After a brief stint picking strawberries on a farm in Ledbury, we chose to focus purely on delinquency thereafter. Backbreaking menial labour for a pittance of remuneration was a mug's game.

Jon was the archetypal sneak thief. So skinny that his presence in any commercial establishment was barely a rumour, he looked sufficiently anonymous that he could walk out of most high street stores with numerous items of stock secreted on his person. He specialised in books, CDs and alcohol but also became adept at stealing cheque books and banker's cards from the back rooms of local shops. The cheque books were always in female names in order that Emma could pass herself off as the account holder. Throughout the illicit pact, I neither stole a cheque nor signed one but there is little doubt that I was the ringleader and had no objection to counting the receipts.

By now I had constructed a robust belief system in defence of my behaviours. Any person with the faintest vestige of gumption would report a stolen cheque book immediately thus avoiding financial liability. Consequently, it was the banks who would take the hit. Banks were intrinsically bad because they were corporate capitalist wankers with immoral business interests in places like South Africa. The more I thought about it, we were freedom fighters, cocking a snook at society whilst we allowed our creative talents to ferment.

The best way to maximise revenue, I determined, was to head to London and cash the cheques in pubs all over the city. The early 90s were a fraudster's paradise with electronic commerce in its infancy and cheques still the most popular form of alternative payment besides cash. It wasn't uncommon for bar staff to honour a cheque up to £50 for a perfect stranger on the premise that the money would be handed back over the bar in due course. Jon would often wait outside as Emma and I entered the pub and made our polite enquiry, appearing every inch an affluent young couple from the suburbs. If the response was affirmative then she would order a round and pocket the change before we downed the drinks and headed for the next licensed premises. In the event of a 'knock back', we would leave immediately. Outside of central London, where publicans were naturally suspicious, the strike rate was about 1 in 4. I couldn't think of anything conceptually better then getting rich whilst getting drunk in my favourite city.

On the very first kiting spree in the metropolis, we were on the lookout for ecstasy. Jon had never tried it and there was still a sense that he was being initiated into the gang. After a good day's work, we were strolling through the Soho darkness when a powerfully built black man approached and asked, "Are you guys looking for somewhere to go…?" I told him we were looking for 'Es' and he said he would take us to a place where we could score. We walked for a few blocks and I made small talk until we came to a shady establishment on Brewer Street called 'The Pink Panther Bar.' In truth It was no kind of bar at all. We followed our tour guide up two flights of stairs before arriving at what resembled a seedy mini cab office in which a pair of foreign girls and a young man of Maltese appearance were watching a tiny black and white television set. R.E.M's 'Losing My Religion' was playing.

We were obliged to buy 3 cans of Carlsberg at £2 a pop and the young man said that the pills would be £20 each. When I suggested the tariff was a bit steep he replied, "It's the West End, man…!" I handed him £60 and the black guy suddenly insisted, "You've got to give me a tenner of that. I brought them here."

"If I give you a tenner then I can't do the deal, "pleaded the 'Maltese Falcon.' I plucked a ten pound note from my pocket as if it were Monopoly money and gave it to our mediator before taking the 3 off white tablets and getting up to leave. "Those arseholes are taking the piss out of me," bemoaned the black guy as he escorted us back onto the street.

Jon came up outside Burger King, just as a big fight erupted between two ethnic factions in Leicester Square and police converged on the scene. Within half an hour, we were all rushing our heads off and spent the next few hours flitting around Piccadilly, China Town and Mayfair. Despite being relatively pricey, the pills had saved us the cost of a hotel for the night, at least. As the dawn rose, we caught a night bus to Kingston and, from there, a taxi towards Richmond. Noticing that we were passing through Ham, I decided it would be a wonderful idea to pay Andy and Emma a visit. Quite what possessed me to knock up a married couple at 6.30am on a weekday is anyone's guess but it certainly resulted in swift and harsh rebuttal. With Blade in no mood for socialising we ended up catching a few hours sleep on the river bank in the early morning sun. Emma warned Jon to immerse himself in the shade since ecstasy users who fell asleep in the sun had been known to 'go mad.' It seemed like a case of shutting the door after the horse had bolted to me.

And so it went, for the remainder of '93 and the first part of the New Year. We lived from one cheque book run to another and if Jon wasn't hitting necessary 'quotas' then I duly scolded him. I imagined myself a romantic figure but was actually a controlling, deluded petty criminal - too afraid of life to maximise my potential. Fuelled by my voracious reading of underworld history, I soon acquired a pin striped, double breasted suit, some fitted white shirts and a garish Marilyn Monroe tie. As I swaggered between Gloucester and London - first class - swigging Jack Daniels with pockets full of dishonest cash, I fancied myself as a dandy version of Reggie Kray.

As with any other endeavour, we learned our trade by trial and error. Central London and the East End were generally too hot but the outskirts, particularly West London, were fertile ground. Fullers Inns, abundantly found in Richmond and Chiswick, were best of all due to a company policy to cash any cheque with a banker's card up to fifty pounds. We invested in a London pub guide and must have given every Fuller's house in the capital the benefit of our degeneracy.

Throughout this time, we scored gear at least twice a week via

Chris and Tash. Jon was using, too, but none of us betrayed any signs of getting a habit. Becoming physically addicted to heroin takes a lot longer than the average person might think. Seminal junky writer, William Burroughs, once contended that a user needed to inject twice a day for 3 months in order to get 'any kind of habit at all.' I didn't know about that but you can certainly smoke the stuff on a casual basis for quite a while before experiencing any withdrawal symptoms.

During this period, Jon also forged a romance with Jenny's younger sister, Laura. She would have been 14 when the dalliance began but things probably didn't progress in the carnal sense until she was 15. Jon was only 18 himself, it should be remembered. Laura was entering that typically rebellious phase and it's not hard to understand why she might have been attracted to my handsome new sidekick who spoke of Larkin and Keats. For his part, he fell hopelessly in love and soon became obsessively jealous and dictatorial. The honeymoon period of our dynamic was over and some of his idiosyncrasies were becoming harder to ignore.

On one occasion, we ventured to Oxford on a Saturday afternoon in search of new pastures for our deceptions. Jon's extensive knowledge of his old 'Varsity' town might come in handy, I reasoned. Within an hour it became painfully obvious to me that he had never previously set foot in the city. If he was lying about that then what else might he have been dishonest about..? I came to understand that he would lie reflexively and apparently without logical motive. The straw that broke the camel's back from Emma's perspective came when she asked if he might have any bowls or plates in his room. Vehemently, he swore there were none. Somewhat puzzled at the lack of ceramics in the kitchen, she eventually searched his bedroom and discovered a generation of crockery, bizarrely wrapped in newspaper and bound with string. We weren't going to live with this freak anymore, she said.

I don't want to give the reader a bad impression. Jon was essentially a good person. One could see the innate decency, tunnelling under the walls of emotional baggage and dysfunction. From a practical standpoint, however, it was never going to emerge within an agreeable time frame.

11/ LOVE AND MARRIAGE

Upon moving back to Stroud, Emma was the first to get a methadone prescription. We were renting a 2 bed roomed house on Horns Road from an old family acquaintance of hers and our mutual opiate addiction came on in leaps and bounds in the skag sodden valley. Actually, methadone is not an opiate as such but a powerfully addictive drug in its own right. It cured nothing besides the urgent need to rob and pillage in pursuit of a fix but it was cheap and suited to mass production. A very determined person might occasionally make a success of a short term methadone reduction plan but many addicts had nothing to look forward to beyond a lifetime of liquid maintenance or an 'upgrade' to diamorphine. If neither one of us had a physical habit at the outset of this new regime then we certainly acquired a problem after several weeks of sharing her weekly allotment of the sugary green solution and topping up with street gear.

Wednesday was methadone day in Stroud and every self respecting smack head would be standing in line at 9am at the hospital dispensary waiting for their various dosages depending on the severity of habit. Or at least depending on whatever they had told Dr. Bailey, the curmudgeonly old cow who had sole tyranny over such things. The average starting 'script' was 25 milligrams a day or 175 mils a week. Critics of the system pointed to the folly of giving a drug addict anything on a weekly basis and expecting them to limit their daily consumption. Some likened it to handing an alcoholic a bottle of whisky and asking him to take two spoonfuls a day. Certainly, a lot of users would exhaust their supply within 48 hours or simply sell it as soon as they got it.

Despite this continued descent into addiction, 1994 was a progressive year from a musical standpoint. I was regularly socialising with Roland again who had agreed to be our mentor and manager. For those familiar with the genealogy of our friendship, he was essentially ousted from Centurion Vintners shortly after my dismissal and now managed a gentleman's outfitters in Cheltenham. Under his stewardship, things began to move forward. Initially, we rehearsed with a young trio from Gloucester but Roland was of the view that they weren't up to the job. Consequently, I teamed up with 'Mac', an older lead guitarist and something of a local celebrity on the band scene. Mac could really play and had a credible background, having nearly made it to the bigger league whilst fronting a four piece called 'The Things.' He was also a heroin addict but I probably saw that as a plus point at the time.

Mac brought in Johnny 'Sticks', a highly competent drummer who had provided the backbeat for 'Spies In The Sugar', a popular soul covers band on the local circuit in my teenage years. Since we couldn't find a suitable bass player, Roland stepped up using a cheap black Marlin we had purchased months earlier on a kiting binge in London. After a few weeks of rehearsal, we were ready to launch our assault. I named the band 'Junky' in homage to William Burroughs' iconic novel, which didn't endear me to my ever present detractors in town.

Junky played its first gig in October '94 at the prestigious Gloucester Guildhall, sharing the bill with retro punk band, Titanic, and a grunge trio by the name of Kick. Before we went on, Mac, Emma and I openly chased heroin in the dressing room causing the other bands to flee in search of a safe haven in which to smoke their spliffs. When the singer of Titanic wasn't being a pop star, he worked as a bin man and I would later hear from Neil - who was also engaged in refuse collection at the time - that he had been rather impressed by such brazen behaviour.

Even by the standards of punk rock orthodoxy, our set was a little short, consisting of 3 Andy Blade numbers, a sole original plus a couple of covers via Buzzcocks and The Only Ones respectively. The self penned effort was called 'Drugs for Laura', an ode to her first pill on a Saturday afternoon at the fairground. Unfortunately, Laura was unable to bear witness to this inaugural showcase since Jon had claimed that I didn't want her at the gig. It was, of course, pure fiction based entirely on his need to control and sequester. Still only 16, she had moved in with him by now but was seldom allowed to leave the house, such was his fear of losing her to the outside world. Jon, himself, was present and correct as were Drac,

Jenny and a small contingent of well wishers.

Short or not, our performance went down well with the reasonably sized crowd and everyone was upbeat as we headed backstage, brushing past members of Titanic as they prepared to tread the boards. Actually, I was elated. The carefully crafted identity I had inhabited for the last 5 years suddenly had form and substance. This would be the legendary first gig to which anoraks would refer in years to come. The mood was celebratory in the Guildhall bar as Emma, Roland and I convened with Drac and Jenny for drinks and post recital analysis. At around 10.30pm Drac drove us home after which we smoked some more gear and retired to bed. Our 'Kurt and Courtney' story was in motion, we fancied.

A month later, we got married in an intimate ceremony at Stroud Registry Office with family and friends in attendance. The reception was held in the back bar of The Pelican, literally across the street and perfectly congruous with the alternative ambience. Emma wore a thigh length, pastel yellow dress with a daisy garland and I wore my dark blue cheque fraud suit with a sapphire silk tie. As splendid as we may have looked, Emma's father couldn't hide his disappointment at the public binding of a union of which he had never greatly approved. His only daughter now legally trussed to a life with the narcissistic ne'er do well who had an answer for everything. Addressing the throng with due deference to wedding protocol he conceded:

"I'm so pleased that these two are.... happy. And I sincerely hope that ....henceforth.... they attack life and are not passive about it..."

A distinguished man in his mid 50s, fulfilling his paternal obligation with a bare minimum of goodwill, I actually admired his integrity at that moment. He was right about our collective inability to attack life and blaze a trail. That would have required the courage to come out of our narcotic bunker. If I had a daughter then I wouldn't want her marrying the 24 year old incarnation of me, either.

For his part, Dad provided an upbeat antithesis to the teeth gritted pleasantries of the Bride's father when his turn came to make an allocution. Emma was the perfect daughter in law, he declared. And what's more, he had known it from the start. He was on top form, perhaps due to the fact I had plied him with amphetamines that very morning. The 'whizz' prevented him from getting drunk and descending into the kind of routines that had seen him shunned from the White Horse or the Red Cow on countless occasions. Mum, who was accompanied by her partner of the time, must have wondered how he hadn't managed to upset anyone by mid afternoon,

The usual suspects were in the house, including Drac and Jenny - despite the former having been released from a mental institution less than 24 hours earlier following a suicide attempt. During my speech, I joked that my brother had been installed as Best Man due to the colourful unpredictability of my closest male friends. By 5pm, it was time to climb into a vintage Jaguar and head for our honeymoon in the Malvern Hills. Despite the old man's reluctance, Emma's parents had paid for us to spend the weekend at a boutique hotel, specifically in a self contained annexe known as 'The Cottage in the Wood.' The icing on the cake was the presentation of a silver grey credit card with instructions to enjoy but 'don't go mad.'

My first priority upon entering our conjugal suite was to get stuck into the bag of gear I had purchased from Mac earlier in the day although Emma was less than overjoyed at my disinterest in her carefully selected lingerie. I was so inherently inconsiderate that it wouldn't have occurred to me to make a fuss of the new Mrs. Doughty in these lavish surroundings. If wasn't as if she was a virgin bride, at any rate. If that sounds unromantic then it's only fair to say that we were both rather cock a hoop with glee to be married and spent much of the weekend beaming at one another as we ordered attractively served nouveau cuisine in the grand hotel restaurant. Returning to Horns Road on the Monday evening, I discovered that Dad - whilst house sitting in our absence - had found my speed stash and snorted the lot. From what I could gather, he had made quite an impression in the Pelican while he was at it.

We played our second and final gig as 'Junky' in February '95 at the Maltings Nightclub in Stroud. There were bad vibes in the camp on account of my belief that Mac had sold a cheap Stratocaster I had lent him over Christmas, in order to feed his habit. He claimed that the axe had gone missing from our rehearsal space at The Pelican but I was more inclined to believe in the tooth fairy. If the first performance had been a triumph then the sequel was palpably dire. Roland had a bizarre off night in the key of Z minor and we were decidedly upstaged by the support band who not only brought most of the crowd but duly took it with them before our second song concluded.

We hacked our way through the remainder of the set for the delectation of our nearest and dearest but their polite applause did nothing to ease the sense of deflation. It felt like losing a fight in the ring, only worse.

The desultory gig notwithstanding, we still had enough impetus to record a demo tape that Roland sent to the likes of Rough Trade and Food. To my faint surprise, neither label summoned us to an exclusive Camden restaurant with their cheque books at the ready. Looking back, I didn't have the faintest clue what it took to make it in the music business. Perhaps I genuinely believed that 2 gigs and a half decent demo would be sufficient.

Summer came, the band imploded and Laura made good her escape from Jon's intolerable clutches. He had thought they were moving to London on the week in question but, waiting for her captor to attend some crucial errand in town; she seized her worldly possessions and jumped in a taxi to Horns Road. Emma wasn't wildly excited about having an attractive female in the house for an indefinite period but Laura was my surrogate little sister and that was that. Whilst she was under our roof, there was no possibility that Jon would bother her. He must have felt helpless and alone.

By now, Emma and I were using gear intravenously. 'Banging up' offered a more intense high than chasing the dragon and we had both overcome any former queasiness about the process. As we upped the stakes in a dangerous game, any attempts to get a new band together came to nothing. As much as I espoused Sex, Drugs and Rock N' Roll, it was clear that I could do without the Rock N' Roll if push came to shove. As for sex, my arrangements were about to change in that regard, too.

12/ ANOTHER GIRL, ANOTHER PLANET

The worst thing about junk sickness is the insomnia. I never experienced the more gruesome aspects of withdrawal described by lifelong junkies. I knew neither diarrhoea nor hair trigger orgasms but simply couldn't sleep when I was 'clucking.' Consequently, I would toss and turn all night, experimenting with a thousand different positions, strangely convinced that each new placement of my restless limbs would provide the tranquillity that eluded me. Finally, I'd had enough.

In junkie circles, a promise to get clean carries about as much clout as the Iranian Rial. Frequently, I would find myself in local drug dens, listening to half a dozen smack heads at once, expounding on their plans to go to rehab or detox - after which they would join the foreign legion or the Muslim Ministry. But despite the lack of encouraging precedents, I was utterly convinced that I could kick the habit with sheer determination and grit. After all, was it really so different to roadwork or making weight...?

In a few weeks, I reduced my methadone dosage from 25 mils a day to 20 and then from 20 to 15 and so on. After hitting the 10 mil mark, I was no longer stoned on a daily basis and my libido was starting to kick in. Unfortunately, Emma was heading in the opposite direction, not only failing to cut down but consuming all the excess that I wasn't using on a weekly basis. Previously we had done everything together or not at all: We lived together, sang together, took drugs and broke the law together. But now came a fork in the road and things got worse when Graham got out of rehab.

Graham was a virtuoso bass player and the quintessential poster boy addict. An affably comical character who had a dysfunctional relationship with just about everything, himself included. Speed was his favoured poison but he also took heroin and a 6 month, court ordered stint in a Wiltshire rehabilitation facility had failed to cure his chronic compulsions. As the autumn of 1995 drew in, we moved to a charmingly cavernous cottage In Nailsworth, 4 and a half miles from Stroud and its innumerable dealers. It would be a better environment in which to get clean, I reasoned.

For the last 2 weeks of my independent methadone reduction programme, I used an oral syringe to administer ever decreasing dosages. Then, after squirting a paltry 2 milligrams into my mouth for a few days on the spin, I stopped taking 'The Juice' altogether. Remarkably, I still experienced mild withdrawal symptoms for the next 5 days thereafter. An ordinary person wouldn't notice 2 mils in their system but the same minuscule amount could keep a junkie from climbing the walls.

Mission duly accomplished, I spent much of my time jamming in the lounge and working on new songs with Graham, during amphetamine benders that might go on for 48 hours at a time. Liberal amounts of Special Brew were consumed to counteract the desolate speed comedowns and my sleep patterns were highly irregular. It didn't occur to me that excessive adherence to any particular substance might point to the same inherent malady. I just assumed that heroin didn't agree with me. Renouncing drugs in their entirety would have seemed like throwing out the baby with the bath water. I would continue to party in Bacchanalian fashion whilst merely avoiding the 'brown.'

During this time, Emma and I clashed frequently. We bickered over her inability and reluctance to get off the gear but it was deeper than that. After nigh on 4 years, she was rebelling against the oppressive control I had exerted over every aspect of her being. Her music taste, her 'opinions', her dress sense and personal style. Increasingly, as she sought to jettison me from her life, she forged an alliance with Graham and I began to feel like a pariah in my own home. Although I could see them becoming thick as thieves, I never imagined they would effectively run away together. Graham was ginger, balding and rather odd, for want of a better word. How could he possibly usurp me in anything remotely dependent on aesthetics and charisma...?

My sustaining arrogance prevented me from noticing an affair that was being conducted right under my nose.

2 days before Christmas, Emma and I had a blazing row in which terrible epithets were issued on both sides. I awoke on Christmas Eve to find she had gone. I could scarcely believe her effrontery as my mind raced through the possibilities as to where she might be. I figured she had probably headed for her parents' new home in Shropshire but I didn't know the landline number and the only people of my acquaintance who had mobile phones in this era were drug dealers. I asked Drac if he would drive me the 70 miles to Onibury but, quite rightly, he declined and told me I would have to take it on the chin and see if she came back.

I've had a surprising number of dreadful Yuletides and Christmas '95 remains up there with the worst of them. I languished in the cottage alone, quaffing cans of Special Brew and allowing every stimulus to remind me of her. It didn't seem fair to have liberated myself from the hand to mouth misery of heroin dependence only to fall victim to such an egregious betrayal. Accepting any portion of the blame for this sorry situation was not a credible option.

The day after Boxing Day, she duly returned with no explanation, playing her cards close to the chest. Initially, I was overjoyed, assuming she had seen the error of her ways but things were worse than before. The final nail in the coffin was her newly dyed pillar box red hair. Now she didn't even look like my Emma. Hostile, flame haired and recalcitrant, she was drawing a final line under something I had thought would last forever. One Sunday evening in early January '96, I walked out of the door and left her and Graham to it. Symbolically, I took nothing besides my guitar and the complete works of Oscar Wilde.

Stepping out into the night, I hitched a lift to Stroud and then walked to the top of town before knocking on the door of the new flat that Jenny and Laura shared at No.1 Stone Manor. Jenny knew my marriage was severely on the rocks and had said I could stay anytime if worst came to the worst. She poured me a glass of wine and invited me into the lounge where the sisters were hosting a small gathering. Back in the neighbourhood where my adult life had begun, I felt as if a monumental weight had been lifted from my shoulders. Emma was a tragic figure, I concluded, and that egg headed, ginger freak was welcome to her. To this day, my advice to anyone in an unhappy relationship is to take a deep breath and let it go.

The conclusion I had dreaded turned out to be a blessing. I got over Emma with ludicrous alacrity and projected my romantic affections onto Jenny, for whom I'd always had a thing. With no property or children to fight over. I simply went to collect the rest of my belongings a couple of days later and that was that. It was obvious that Graham had moved in without delay since his dressing gown hung from the bedroom door, emblematically. Soon they would move to Brighton where she would land a lucrative gig, managing an escort agency. Or so she would claim, at least. Hitherto, the narrative has failed to address that she had a few mental health issues. Formerly 15 stone and full of self loathing, Emma hadn't emotionally adjusted to her new incarnation as an attractive young woman and took a surfeit or mood stabilisers to combat symptoms of depression or bi - polar disorder. Graham was nothing more than the accomplice she needed to escape from the prison that our marriage had become. He wouldn't last long.

In response to anyone who might accuse me of being ethically bankrupt, I ought to stress that Jenny's love life was complicated when I set my sights on her. She had become embroiled in a strange love triangle with Drac and her attractive cousin, Penny, and was evidently becoming weary of the situation. Drac and Penny had found their particular chemistry at a time when he and Jenny were on a break, whilst the latter was living in London, working in bars and indulging a few casual affairs. Upon her return to Stroud, they became an item once more but with Penny still in the picture. Things went as far as a bizarre 'matrimonial' ceremony conducted on Painswick Beacon in which vows were made and rings were exchanged. Penny made a good wage as a chartered accountant, so I'm guessing she bought the 'bands of gold' that were proudly exhibited in the aftermath.

In any case, Jenny wasn't in receipt of Drac's undivided attention when I came to be living under the same roof. In the weeks that followed, we spent a lot of time together, listening to music and putting the world to rights while consuming copious amounts of bass amphetamine. Initially, she parried my non threatening advances but I simply kept trying. One Saturday night in February, not long after my 26th birthday, she capitulated and our platonic love was upgraded to the more complex variety. Predictably, I justified my position on the basis of Drac's infidelity, despite being unsure of the standard protocol in 3 way marriages. The 'Bros Before Hos' maxim was easier to adhere to in principle than in practice, it seemed.

The first half of 1996 was a period of renaissance. If my relationship with Emma had been all about hiding from the world in an opiate fog then Jenny and I were soon stepping out on the town in our finery. It was the era of Brit Pop - Cool Britannia and speed was our drug of choice. Cocaine was for overpaid philistines in jumped up wine bars and trendy nightclubs. 'Whizz' was vastly better for endless weekends of partying and ravenous come down sex. Throughout this time, I continued to write songs and jammed with potential band members. None of these line ups amounted to anything but, somehow, I still saw myself as the poet laureate of the underground in waiting. Especially with a new Rock Queen at my side.

At some point in the spring, Jon got nicked for the burglary of an antiquarian bookshop in Gloucester during which 50 thousand pounds worth of rare books and paintings were allegedly stolen. For several weeks before the crime took place, he had been frequenting the appointment only section of 'Westgate Books', waxing lyrical about W.H Auden whilst slipping the odd fore edge edition into his coat pockets , unbeknownst to the various shop assistants who continued to entertain him. Presumably, they thought he was a literature enthusiast who liked to browse but never actually bought anything. The books he was pilfering were typically priced between £300 - £400 and he was selling them on to a local collector for £75 each. Before long, he happened to relay the details of this lucrative venture to his flat mate, an ex-con who suggested that it would be far more expedient to steal all the books at once.

The heist was a success and so Jon called an urgent rendezvous with the collector at Gloucester train station for around 10pm on a Wednesday night. He was leaving for London forthwith, he claimed, and needed to sell the contents of his dear grandfather's heirloom in their entirety and without delay. One can only imagine how shady the scene must have looked as Jon exchanged several bin liners, chock full of hooky antiquarian literature, for a few thousand pounds tendered by a man in his late 40s, under cover of darkness.

The following day, when news of the robbery hit the front page of the Citizen, John Wright claimed to realise he had been duped and was in possession of stolen goods. It seemed highly probable he had known all along that the books weren't entirely kosher and was simply trying to get himself off the hook. The problem, from Jon's perspective, was that he had given the man his real name. Much of what he had told Mr. Wright had been pure fiction, which was par for the course, but he had not seen fit to give himself an alias. Consequently, he was picked up by the old bill as soon as he returned from the smoke and eventually charged with burglary and handling.

When the trial unfolded at Gloucester Crown Court, I did my bit as a witness for the defence. It was extremely unlikely that my friend had physically partaken in the burglary, I explained, as he was with me for much of the evening in question. The jury must have believed me as Jon was acquitted of burglary but found guilty of handling, for which he was bang to rights. He didn't expect to receive a prison sentence and must have been shocked when the judge announced:

"BURGLARS GO TO PRISON AND THAT'S WHERE YOU'RE GOING.

YOUR CO - CONSPIRATORS MUST KNOW THAT THE SAME FATE AWAITS THEM IN THE EVENT THEY ARE CAUGHT...."

Jon got 6 months, which equated to 3, most of which he served at HMP Exeter. It had taken 3 years since our initial meeting for one of us to end up 'behind the door.' And in the coming months, Jenny and I would come perilously close to following him.

13/ LONDON CALLING

Although I had kicked the physical habit, I was still using heroin on a recreational basis, despite my best intentions. Just after Christmas, I happened to be in The Pelican when I bumped into a French junkie called Alain who asked me, "Do you know where to score BIG...?" It turned out he had received £700 pounds in backdated benefits and was looking to purchase a weighed amount without getting robbed. Not being well liked and respected, even in such a lowly subculture, he had every right to assume that most of the local characters would rip him off as soon as look at him. In truth, I only knew the street level dealers but I wasn't about to let the opportunity slip through my fingers. Especially not when he showed me the folding cash and promised to look after me in the event of a successful brokerage.

By now, I had made my peace with Emma since our divorce and knew that she had a few connections in Brighton. Alain liked the idea of a sojourn and so he, Jenny and I jumped on a train and headed for the South Coast. At this point, it seems relevant to mention that heroin was not the only bad habit I had fallen back into. Shortly before Christmas, a small time local crook had approached me with a stolen chequebook that had come into his possession. I agreed to take it off his hands on the premise that Jenny and I needed money for the festive season. Accordingly, we set about the old routine of passing the cheques in London boozers for a few days while staying at Dad's new flat on Sheen Road. With the New Year nearly upon us, I figured we would plough through the remaining cheques before turning over a new leaf and going straight. As it happened, I would be half right with that projection.

Emma lived alone in a smart flat in Hove, having ditched Graham a few months after the move. As strange as it might have been, she had no issue with Jenny and I being together and happily offered to put us up for the night alongside Alain whom she vaguely knew from Stroud. Scoring 'big' wasn't as straightforward as anyone might have hoped and it was after midnight when we finally got what we came for, courtesy of a dealer who lived on the seafront directly opposite Brighton Pier. As far as the taxi driver was concerned, we were on a late night mission to retrieve a crucially important set of keys. 'The Man' refused to sell in denominations greater than half a gram, so Alain purchased 8 half grams while I waited in the car. He had expected better but still gave me half a gram for my trouble, sighing, "BRI-TON... I weel not forget this town...!" Back at Emma's pad, everyone got stoned before the hostess retired to bed and left us to 'gouch out' on the living room floor.

The next morning, Alain headed back to Stroud under his own steam whilst Jenny and I opted to spend New Year's Eve with my old friend, Nick, who had moved to Brighton a few years prior. We had been close since childhood, as next door neighbours when my family first moved to the Cotswolds back in 1978 but could not have chosen more different pathways in the years that followed. Since the acid trip from hell he had stayed on the straight and narrow. He had a decent job, a mortgage, a pension plan and all of the other things I found so desperately soul destroying and suburban.

If ever there was a day on which I should have stayed in bed it was January 2, 1997. As Jenny stood in the queue at Hove station, I reminded her to include a pair of 1 day travel cards on our tickets since we had no liquid cash and Victoria was too hot for kiting. Unfortunately, by the time she got served at the kiosk, she had forgotten my precise instructions. Now, we would need to cash at least one dodgy cheque in SW1 in order to facilitate our travel to the suburbs. It was an oversight that would cost us dearly.

Arriving in Victoria an hour later, we suffered one refusal after another until a wine bar called 'Vino Veritas' relented to cash us a cheque for £30. We tried a few more pubs, including 'The Shakespeare' and 'The Bag O' Nails', without success, before I decreed that we should get the hell out of Central London. En route to the tube station, I stopped to buy a tuna mayonnaise baguette from a nearby sandwich bar. As we attempted to purchase our travel cards from one of the ticket machines, we were suddenly surrounded by a gang of plain clothes police officers, one of whom proffered his badge and declared, "TRANSPORT POLICE…!"

I couldn't think of any plausible reason why they might be following us and my knee jerk reaction was to shout, "RUN, JEN…!" I tried in vain to follow my own advice but the ringleader cop, who bore a striking resemblance to 'Tosh' from 'The Bill', barred my way. Half a tuna baguette in my left hand, I hit him squarely in the mouth with a straight right, which achieved nothing besides an instant lack of leniency on the part of his colleagues who set about me. Bizarrely, 'Tosh' grabbed me by the testicles and enquired 'Hard man, yeah…? You want some…?" As I was taken to the ground, they ordered me to 'Drop the sandwich,' although I steadfastly refused to do so. Irked by this gesture of defiance, they yelled loudly in unison, "DROP THE SANDWICH….! PUT IT DOWN…!" I took one last stubborn bite of my lunch before it was wrested from the grip and the formal caution was given. The scene must have looked highly comical to the random spectators left wondering what was precisely so illegal and threatening about a tuna mayonnaise baguette.

'Tosh' was bleeding slightly and not at all happy as they lead us away in handcuffs. "You made a mistake back there," he assured me. "As soon as we get you where the public can't see you, we can do what we like… You're right to look worried…!"

"I'm not worried. I just want to know that the fuck this is all about," I shot back.

Initially, they took us to the Transport Police office in Victoria Station for preliminary interrogation, in separate rooms to prevent any collusion between us. To begin with, I claimed to be the husband of the woman named on the chequebook since I was still wasn't sure if 'Plod' even knew why they had arrested us. My ruse fell at the first fence as Jenny had evidently given her real name and I was clutching at straws, in any case. It turned out that the undercover team had chosen to tail us at random due to our irregular movements, walking in and out of numerous pubs in such a short space of time. They had actually assumed that we were professional bag thieves and not fraudsters at all. My deathly white countenance and lack of an overcoat in January was allegedly a contributory factor in drawing the heat. It was basically the policing equivalent of a 'lucky punch.' I told them they were 'jammy bastards' and held my hands up.

The mood suddenly lightened and even 'Tosh' became friendly and gregarious. "Nice to have met you," he said before making tracks to wherever a 'Tosh' lookalike might be required in the fight against crime. I apologised for punching him in the face not 15 minutes ago, to which he replied, "I'd have done the same…. Only I'd have kept on fighting….!" The team dispersed and we were left in the care of one D.C Millward and another officer who transported us to the nearby Belgravia Police Station in the back of a Met Van. Duly booked in and reminded of our right to legal representation, we endured the customary hours of solitary boredom until they were ready to interview us.

As annoyed as I was at getting caught in such slapstick fashion, I didn't suppose it was the end of the world. Jenny had no previous and it was my first offence of this nature. The worst we could be looking at was 6 months probation and a fine. Unfortunately, explained Millward and his mate, there were complications. They had been on the phone to the Stroud constabulary who alluded to a rash of incidents over the last 3 years involving chequebooks stolen from Stroud and Gloucester and cashed in pubs all over London by a man and a woman vaguely matching our description. It seemed highly likely, they suggested, that the masterminds of a long standing criminal enterprise were currently in their custody. They were half right in that assumption, of course, but I was damned if I would see Jenny go down for Emma's misdeeds. On the plus side, my striking of the officer at the scene was never mentioned again.

We both denied all knowledge of any previous offences and simply owned up to the chequebook and cards we had been caught with. To compound a thoroughly bad day, the landlord of the Slad Road studio flat into which we had recently moved was aghast to receive a call from the Metropolitan Police seeking to verify a bail address and terminated our tenancy on the spot. Millward appeared to take great delight in telling me, "You don't live there anymore...!" Luckily - if that is the right word - Dad agreed to his address being used and we were released at around 10pm on unconditional bail, with orders to return in 6 weeks time. As we curled up on the old man's floor that night there seemed precious little to be cheerful about. Certainly, I felt a twinge of guilt for putting Jenny in such a wretched situation. On reflection, it was hardly surprising that Emma's father hadn't regarded me as ideal son in law material.

The next day, Jon was released from Exeter Jail, which couldn't have been timelier as he was by far the best bet for a place to stay while we pondered our next move. Thanks to the welfare state, he still had a home to come back to at 72 Linden Road and predictably welcomed us with open arms. Being flat broke after our misfortune, I had to borrow money from Dad for the train fares back to Gloucester. Upon arrival, I discovered that Jon had been neither hardened nor reformed by his brief stint at Her Majesty's Pleasure but had gained weight because he liked the prison food. Despite his fears at the outset, the whole experience of incarceration had been a 'piece of piss' he said.

He had a dodgy landlord at Linden Road, a former Justice of the Peace who was later struck off for some kind of scurrilous behaviour that the tabloids got hold of. His name was Dave and he suggested that Jenny and I take one of the spare rooms in the building and claim housing benefit. 2 weeks later, he changed his mind and withdrew the offer when I burned down the kitchen during a late night misadventure with the fat fryer. 1997 had started badly and seemed to be getting worse. We had little choice, I concluded, than to put our things in storage and head back to London in search of a new life.

14/ TO LIVE AND DIE IN RICHMOND

Before we left town, PC Andrews and O'Brien at Stroud Police Station wanted a word with us about a blizzard of similar crimes to the one with which we would inevitably be charged in a few weeks time. Andrews was a cold, clinical bastard from North of the border who fancied that he would not let his prey off the hook. O'Brien was a moderately attractive blonde in her mid to late 20s and seemed less invested in the whole affair. The duty solicitor requisitioned to our assistance was one Howard Ogden, who had recently returned from a suspension for professional misconduct relating to his relationship with former client and serial murderer, Fred West. I got the impression he didn't like coppers, which meant he was ok by me.

Andrews alluded to the existence of a draw on the premises containing a ream of embezzled cheques and suggested that my fingerprints might be found on some of them. I stood firm and told him I would be astonished if that were the case. I was, I continued, a morally upstanding citizen who had been tragically tempted in a moment of madness at a fiscally demanding time of year. I made much of the argument that the varied descriptions of Emma sounded nothing like Jenny and suggested that any further grilling would be tantamount to harassment.

Howard Ogden agreed that there no hard evidence to justify our further detainment. I was returned to a cell while Jenny was interviewed but wasn't unduly concerned, knowing that she was entirely innocent in the first place. An hour later, we were both released without charge and ready to bid the old town farewell.

Dad's circumstances had changed, making him even more reluctant to entertain houseguests than he had been previously. According to his version of events, he had temporarily relocated to a 'holiday flatlet' the size of a horse box on Queens Road while refurbishments were carried out at the Sheen Road pad. It might have been true but I had the feeling there was something he wasn't telling me. Something that related to his inability to stay consistently sober and maintain an upward trajectory in life. Either way, the reality was that Jenny and I would have to sleep on the floor of a tiny room that contained a single bed and the bare essentials of a kitchen. I fully imagined that Anne Frank had more elbow room during the composition of her diary but at least there was no danger of us getting too comfortable with the arrangement.

With no time to lose, I started busking immediately and was happy to discover that I could earn ten pounds an hour without breaking sweat. 5 years on from my first flirtation with the District Line, I was now a considerably better singer and guitarist having been seasoned by the Paris and Amsterdam campaigns. Occupational hazards remained in the form of jobsworth drivers, disgruntled passengers and occasional undercover police officers but it seemed plausible that I could net £250 a week whilst not subjecting my vocal chords to undue stress and exhaustion. Within a week, Jenny was working as a barmaid at The Ram, a riverside pub off Kingston High Street and we quickly found a house share in Broom Road, near Hampton Wick Station. Our housemates were a pair of unemployed hippy types who spent much of their time smoking weed, drinking supermarket label vodka and waiting for one another's giro days to come around. Things were on the up.

In late February, we reported to Belgravia Police Station to be charged with theft by deception and bailed to appear at Horseferry Road Magistrates Court in April. In the meantime, we would seek to amass the trappings of normality, thus presenting ourselves as reformed characters when the day of judgement arrived. It was Andy who had helped us find the house that wasn't too far from his new abode by Teddington Lock. The previous summer, Emma had given birth to their first child, Imogen, and quit work to become a full time mother. Blade was now working as an English teacher at a Surbiton Comprehensive, having gone back to University to get his degree. Considering his notoriously threadbare school attendance in the 70s, the situation was not without irony. Although their days of marital bliss were numbered, they appeared as idyllically situated as ever, playing happy families in the Surrey countryside.

Unfortunately, Dad was slightly less well situated as he continued to zigzag between monastic fitness and alcoholic insanity. It was always the same story: Several weeks (or months) of abstinence and good behaviour followed by a relapse during which any semblance of respectability went flying out of the window. He could literally pass for a high end executive one week and a park bench drinker the next. As ever, I didn't appreciate the gravity of the situation and simply welcomed the boozy bonhomie of his typical 3 week benders.

During one such bender in the spring, he needed a cover story to explain his absence from a senior sales position at UK Waste Solutions. Any number of reasonable excuses would probably have sufficed but, for reasons best known to himself, he chose to inform the relevant authority that I was in a diabetic coma. Being as they were, a compassionate company, the top brass insisted he take as long a sabbatical as might be required under such fictitiously awful circumstances.

For the next week or so, my alleged condition fluctuated between critical and stable as he attempted to gauge how many more days he might spend guzzling white cider and watching Sonny Liston documentaries on VHS. Then one afternoon, as I entered his claustrophobic quarters, he broke the 'tragic' news:

"You might want to keep your head down. You're supposed to dead."

That might have been the end of a tasteless farce but the good people of UK Waste, a couple of whom had briefly made my acquaintance, wanted to send a floral tribute. Quite unprepared for awkward questions about where I would be laid to rest, Dad suggested that they send it to his address. It seemed increasingly surreal when, a couple of days later, a wreath with my name on it turned up in the post with their heartfelt condolences. Still drinking and watching classic fights, the old man placed it on top of the television set and casually remarked that the circular foliage looked rather pleasant.

By early June, he was back on the wagon as Jenny and I prepared to face the music at Horseferry Road. The case had already been adjourned twice and now we were up for sentencing. I was still busking but so far as the court were concerned, I was working for Andy's boyhood friend and former Eater guitarist, Brian 'Chevette', who ran a painting and decorating business. Painter and decorator sounded a lot better to a magistrate's ears than illegal street performer when all said and done. To an extent, it was true as I had been helping him renovate a house on Barnstaple Avenue that Andy and Emma had just moved into. Vouching for my essential decency, I had character references from Chris the Company Director - with whom I had finally buried the hatchet - and Andy Blade the Schoolteacher. In actual fact, he had recently given up the teaching job in favour of opening a record stall in Richmond Market. He just couldn't work for the machine, even if he wasn't raging against it anymore.

On the morning of our day in court, despite the rational logic that we were unlikely to receive a prison sentence, I had a sense of foreboding in my gut. We were still talking about more than 1500 pounds worth of damage to coffers of Midland Bank and our lady brief had warned that playing the drugs card was known to backfire on occasion as magistrates and 'stipes' were becoming increasingly weary of lawless junkies. The fact that she was black was also a concern as I looked at the all white lay bench and wondered if they might harbour a natural bias against her gender and ethnicity.

Sense of foreboding or not, I was still taken back when the Chairman of the bench announced, "You must appreciate that ANY bench would have a custodial sentence in mind when one looks at the scale of these offences and the sophistication with which they were carried out."

My pulse quickened as my mind raced with disjointed thoughts: Had he been talking to PC Andrews at Stroud nick…? Did 'Tosh' tell them about the right hander or was karma simply catching up with me...?

"Is Mr Martin - Doughty drug free at this time...?" asked the Chairman.

"YES," came the reply.

"Is Miss. Fisher drug free at this time...?"

Again, the response was affirmative.

"Well, in that case, you rather tie our hands but we are going to consider our verdict," he said as the trio of moral bastions stood up and walked off stage. What did that mean..? He appeared to imply that if the pair of us had been chronically strung out then perhaps they could have sent us to rehab. If we were clean, however, then it would have to be prison after all. Where was the fucking logic in that...? Jenny began to cry softly. None of this had been her fault, after all. I had nothing except, "Jen, we'll be out in 3 months just like Jon was. I love you...."

After a few minutes of deliberation the Chairman and his wingers returned and took their seats once more. He milked the silence before he spoke:

"We are forever seeing people like you before us and we are always assured that the whole world is going to change on Monday morning......

Well, in your case, we're going to see if the world DOES change on Monday morning. We are deferring sentence for 6 months."

I felt like buying him a bottle of Krug champagne. The wanker had tried to scare us but I loved him anyway...! Now, all I had to do was stay out of trouble for 6 months and pretend to be a painter and decorator. We were dismissed from the dock and I thanked our solicitor for her efforts. The whole thing wasn't over yet but we were free to enjoy the summer and the likelihood of losing our liberty seemed more remote than ever. I had no more appetite for skulduggery and genuinely wanted to fly straight from here on in

The irony of choosing Kingston as an area in which to turn over a new leaf was that the town had a notorious smack problem, every bit as bad as the culture that afflicted Stroud. The scene revolved around a drugs project on the outskirts of the town centre called the Kaleidoscope and there were constant police operations and 'swoops' attempting to round up the more prolific dealers. Indeed, recent publicity boasted that 27 such dealers were no longer on the street due to the tireless efforts of the Drug Squad. Nonetheless, there were plenty willing to take their place. Unable to leave it alone, we had sought out a few contacts within weeks of arriving and were still using on a casual basis.

2 days after our result in court, Andy hosted a housewarming party and was visibly annoyed when Jenny and I turned up 'pinned.' Admittedly, his disappointment would have been easier to digest had his own stance on heroin not been so inconsistent. Often, he would veer between paternalistic sermons on the evils of hard drugs and covert trips to the Kingsnympton Park Estate to score a couple of bags from a Dickensian scallywag of my association. Sometimes we would smoke the gear in the shed at the bottom of his garden while Emma played with the baby, blissfully unaware of such sordid iniquity. But it was safe to say he disapproved of any heroin use in which he was not directly involved.

In the first week of December, we returned to Horseferry Road and were ordered to pay compensation. No probation, no community service and no fine as such. Just an order to give back the money we had stolen in whatever minuscule instalments were deemed affordable. In the interim, my prints had turned up on numerous cheques in the name of a young man from Stroud who had actually been in on the scam with me. I had feared it would affect me adversely due to the conditions of the deferred sentence but the Stroud court remitted the case to London and my brief successfully argued that the offence was 'ancient history.' The stipendiary magistrate admitted she was 'quite impressed' with the fact we had kept out trouble for 6 months and, whilst considering us 'very lucky' to have gotten a deferred sentence in the first place, she was not in a punitive mood.

Jenny and I breathed a collective sigh of relief that the 11 month saga was over, knowing full well that we could scarcely have received more clemency. As we left the court for the last time, I swore, "Nothing is going to ruin Christmas this year...!" As cruel fate would have it, I might just as well have saved my breath.

On Saturday December 13, 1997, Dad should have been on a date with an attractive female colleague at the company's regional Christmas bash. Romance was in the air but the deleterious effects of a seasonal bender had left him in no fit state to drive when the fateful evening arrived. Attempting to put on a suit whilst searching for his most buoyant hairpiece, he took copious gulps from a bottle of 'White Lightning' and played for time. Twice In close succession, he answered the telephone and tried to sound perfectly sober:

"On my way now, babe. See you in about 20 minutes...."

On the third occasion, I motioned for him to stay quiet and picked up the receiver myself:

"Hello... This is Joe's son, Ben. I'm afraid that my Dad has a high fever and is in a state of delirium tonight. He keeps talking about an important date with a radiantly beautiful woman, bless him, but I can't possibly allow him to leave the house in this condition. I'll get him to bell you tomorrow it he perks up.."

"Did she buy it...?" he wondered.

"I think so but you had better come up with something fucking convincing on Monday," I warned him.

I had come over because I was hoping to watch Ryan Rhodes challenge Otis Grant for the WBO Middleweight title on Sky Sports. Now we could watch the fight together and drink to our hearts' content. As nice as his jilted date had sounded on the phone, I suspect it was his preferred scenario. He hated missing a big fight for any reason whatsoever. Ultimately, the 21 year old Rhodes was too green for the slick, seasoned Canadian despite the closeness of the official scorecards. I could tell from Frank Warren's body language at ringside that he knew his charge had lost and said as much before the verdict was announced. Dad stood up and gave me a tight hug, saying, "Son, nobody understands fights like you do. I think the bloody world of you and I want you to know that…" In my emotionally reserved way, I told him it was eminently mutual before saying goodnight and catching the R68 back to Teddington. It was the last time I ever saw him alive.

2 days later; unable to get hold of Dad on the phone, I gained entrance to the apartment building and forced my way into his room. As I pushed the door open, he fell face down on the floor, completely motionless. To begin with, I wasn't unduly alarmed, having seen him in similar states on numerous occasions over the years. I started to wash up and gave him a playful kick, using the nickname his mad alcoholic father had often referred to him by.

"C'mon Colonel…! Look lively and greet the new day."

Something in the lack of response caused me to take a closer look and I suddenly realised that his body was half cold and there were rivulets of blood coming from his nostrils. He didn't appear to be breathing. Frantically, I dialled the number for The Ram and demanded to speak to Jenny. When she came to the phone, I half wailed, "I'VE LOST MY DAD….!" before asking her to phone an ambulance and come at once. Around 20 minutes later, the paramedics confirmed what I already knew. "There's nothing we can do the for the gentleman," Surveying the empty cans and bottles that littered the tiny room, one of them said, "I think the drink finally got to him but it's a sudden death so we have to inform the police."

Jenny arrived just in time to see Dad's corpse being carried down the stairs and, shortly afterwards, 2 police officers attended the scene. They were terribly nice and, having briefly spoken to the ambulance men, did not regard the circumstances as suspicious. They offered their condolences and left us to gather our thoughts.

It seemed so inglorious for him to have expired in such threadbare accommodation and the posters of Hagler, Duran and Sugar Ray suddenly looked unbearably poignant now that their owner had left this mortal coil at the tender age of 50. My musings were interrupted when the phone rang. It was Caruna, his intended date from Saturday night.

"Hello, I was just checking that Joe is ok. Is he feeling better..?"

"Hi Caruna. Unfortunately, he's not ok. In fact, I'm very sorry to tell you that he's dead."

Less than 48 hours ago, I had been spinning this woman a yarn about Dad being under the weather and now I was solemnly informing her of his sudden demise. Given that I had alluded to the need for a convincing alibi on Monday, I like to think he would have seen the funny side of it.

The well attended funeral took place on Monday the 22nd of December at Mortlake Crematorium with a wake at the Duke's Head. 3 days before Christmas, the bar was garishly bedecked with festive decorations as many of Dad's old friends from London and the North West regaled one another with funny stories of his trademark shenanigans. When the last of the stragglers left at around 8pm, it suddenly occurred to me that at least a handful of mourners had previously thought that I, too, was dead. Some had even donated to the office whip round to purchase an ornamental wreath back in the summer. Lord knows what they had made of the sight of me emerging from the darkened limo several hours ago but, clearly, they were too polite to mention such things at a traditionally sombre occasion.

15/ 3 DUCKS PEOPLE

In the New Year, we went to stay with my cousin Deborah and her future husband in Hanwell. If the tragedy had a positive side, it was certainly found in the closeness I forged with Deb and Aunt Jane now that Dad was gone. Her other half, Malcolm, was an extremely likeable character and they both made us feel welcome. Observing their dynamic, I began to wonder if suburban life was so terrible after all. There was nothing wrong with living in a nice house and having enough money to go on holiday 2 or 3 times a year. It was surely preferable to opiate addiction, getting arrested or drinking oneself to death.

Nevertheless, I was drinking on a daily basis at this point, a fact Deb and Malcolm would have struggled to ignore as their booze collection dwindled incrementally. It was hard to maintain enthusiasm for the endless performances between Kew Gardens and Hammersmith whilst stone cold sober and so I would sip cans of lager throughout the day before finishing up with a couple of pints in the Flickr and Firkin where I counted the spoils. Upon my return to Ealing, I would hit the liquor cabinet, imbibing whisky or vodka until bedtime.

The plan was for Jenny and me to stay for a couple of months and save a deposit for a new flat in a different part of London. I had my heart set on Ladbroke Grove although Deb opined that we couldn't afford to live in such a trendy, desirable area. Despite her reasonable scepticism, 10 weeks later we moved into a small studio at 152 Ladbroke Grove, a stone's throw from the Tube station. I told the Iranian landlord that I worked in a recording studio in Shepherds Bush since I didn't imagine he would have let the place to a full time busker.

Having moved on a Friday night, with Deb and Malcolm's crucial assistance, we took a stroll the next morning in our fabulous new neighbourhood. The vibrancy of Portobello Road market with its sensory overload of music, food and fashion was hugely inspiring to both of us. This was real London in all of its glory, bearing no resemblance to the South West London backwaters. When we stopped at a local watering hole for a celebratory tipple, there was a mutual sense of optimism after all we had endured. It might have been the first day of the rest of our lives but old behaviours soon reared their ugly heads, in tandem with old acquaintances.

One evening several weeks later, I bumped into Willem coming out of Costcutter with a single can of Foster's in his hand. He had been on a predictably downward spiral since that night almost 7 years ago when he facilitated my first skag deal and was not long out of prison. By his own account, he had stooped to robbing strangers at cash points, armed with a carving knife, before the authorities caught up with him. So far as I could tell he was living in a halfway house in the area and still on probation. Although his emergence didn't spell immediate disaster, I'm quite sure he was a bad omen.

For the next few months, we saw quite a lot of Willem and his girlfriend and before long he introduced me to a pair of local dealers who did home deliveries. Having been reared in the culture of waiting for the man, it was quite a novelty to have a clean cut 'rude boy' arriving punctually at one's door with a 20 pound bag of gear on demand. As had proven to be the case a year earlier, the physical act of moving didn't help to escape the clutches of 'The Beast.'

As the winter encroached, Laura's ex-boyfriend came to stay - supposedly so that he and I could join forces and take the independent music scene by storm. Scott was something of a guitar wizard but - like so many creatives - also suffered with bi polar tendencies, entailing that he was either high as a kite or in the depths of despair. He was into smack and any other drug he could get his hands on. Soon after his arrival, we seemed to know every dealer within a 5 mile radius and even had occasion to score from a man who was said to be Daley Thompson's brother and lived at the top of the Trellick Tower.

Although we did a fair bit of busking, Scott and I had failed to write or record a single song by the time he elected to move back to Bristol in early January. By then, Jenny and I had both acquired injecting habits. When my 29th birthday came around the following month, I took stock of the situation and concluded that another methadone detox was the only sensible course of action. I was tipping the scales at 9 stone 12, the least I had ever weighed in my adult life. 20 minutes skipping in a sweat suit and I could have made lightweight.

Accordingly, we ventured to a clinic in Paddington where they gave out 'scripts' and started on 25 mils a day. It appealed to me that our medicine was dispatched from a pharmacy on Queensway, near the Embassy Hotel from whence Richey Edwards had permanently vanished back in '95. Thankfully, Jenny was equally serious about knocking the gear on the head which made things easier for both of us. Furthermore, we planned to give up the flat as soon as we were drug free, in order to go travelling. Having put our things in storage with her mum, we spent the last week of minor withdrawals at Nick's house in Brighton, whilst he was away on holiday. To keep myself from 'rattling', I would often drink Scotch at 9am in the morning with a couple of Nurofen Plus - a ritual that I failed to identity as a potential problem in itself. I was experiencing that wave of euphoria that some addicts describe when the poison is fully out of their system. So what if I took a few drinks to take the edge off..?

In the second week of April, 1999, we boarded a National Express service to Paris overnight. Arriving at our destination the next morning, we checked into the 3 Ducks Hostel, although I didn't immediately recognise it as the place at which Emma and I had stayed. Having our cards firmly in the alternative guild, we must have assumed that a party hostel would be a good fit. In hindsight, it was a disastrous environment for any couple seeking to resuscitate their relationship.

On the very first night, I regaled the crowded bar with my Brit Pop acoustic repertoire and was immediately surrounded by scores of new friends and well wishers - many of whom were anxious to buy me a drink. It seemed harmless enough at first but with this nightly adulation came female attention that wasn't parried as deftly as it should have been. Jenny and I had pretty much stopped having sex back in London and our carnal axis had yet to recover on foreign soil. Having suppressed my sexual appetite with heroin for months on end, a cocktail of nature's amphetamines and cheap wine juxtaposed with a surfeit of attractive young women from around the globe posed a nagging threat to fidelity.

Despite my self absorption, I had always considered myself the steadfastly faithful type until, one night, a young lady from Virginia suggested that "One kiss wouldn't hurt…" Acquiescing to her desire with appropriate discretion I became instantly intoxicated with the lure of forbidden fruit. When a similar scene unfolded a few nights later with a Dutch girl for whom I had provided an escort to the taxi rank near Place Marcel - Cerdan, it served as confirmation that the plot had been lost. Within a month, Jenny had gotten tired of my brazenly selfish conduct and decided to go back to England for a time out. We hadn't broken up or declared a trial separation but I viewed the situation as a green light to go wild, nonetheless. A one night stand with a guitar strumming songstress from Illinois got me up and running, followed by a brief dalliance with an Australian girl of Asian extraction.

Essentially, I was making up for lost time, having been in a state of continual monogamy for the previous 7 years. At 29, I suddenly had the pulling power I could only have dreamt of back in those awkward days of extended adolescence. As much as I loved Jenny, I had needs and had wasted too much of my 20s in a bubble of drug fuelled elitism.

Busking trips aside, I seldom found an excuse to leave the hostel where my status was at a premium amongst an international cast of characters; Matt the androgynous Aussie barman, Allan the English Kiwi sex god, Jason (a latter day Jackson Pollock), Irish Cathy, ShakesPeter, Jersey Boy Luc and Adamo the Midnight Ninja.

The summer of '99 became a frenzied blur of drinking, carousing and performing - and generally subjecting my liver to the most sustained battering it had yet received. Some of my confederates were a decade younger and couldn't relate to the near death experience hangovers I would describe after 5 or 6 days of unabated consumption. Finding the old man face down in a sea of empty cans and bottles had given me an exaggerated sense of my own mortality but laying off the booze for a few days would not have occurred to me.

The more I partied, the less I was inclined to go out busking and earn my keep. This, in turn, led to the accumulation of a stack of unpaid receipts at the front desk as my familiarity with the staff had allowed me to slip through the net of standard procedure. For several nights in a row I had been afforded a bed on the understanding I would pay later when replete with funds. It was arguably the worst decision in the history of hotel management. At any rate, in an effort to square things with the Moroccan lady supremo, I started working the breakfast shift and went to stay with Sadi, a crazy musician who lived in a family owned apartment around the corner.

Sadi was a fine guitarist and passable singer with some credible recordings to his name but it was also fair to say that he had more issues than the National Newspaper Archive. Although Arabic in appearance, he had grown up in Senegal, a place he hated with a passion that would only allow him to refer to it as 'West Africa.' He once told me that his father had taken him to a pornographic cinema as a child, a spectacle from which he never fully recovered. The fact that he largely subsisted on a diet of rum and cocaine did nothing for his emotional stability.

One night I brought a Canadian girl in her early 20s back to the pad and Sadi gave her a few lines. Emily, who had the lamentable combination of an aesthetically desirable body and low self esteem, went into orbit as she purred, "I'm gonna' become a fucking coke head…! I LIKE this…! Do you guys want me to take my top off…?" In concurrence with a splendid idea, I eased the tight white T - Shirt over her head, revealing pert white breasts, rose tipped. Sadi stood up with a degree of urgency and said, "We have to do this in my room. My mother is sleeping in the spare bedroom." This was news to me although I did recall him alluding to an imminent family visit of some sort. We scurried into the master bedroom, taking Emily and her discarded T - Shirt with us.

In short order; she was relieved of her khaki trousers and black G - String as we snorted lines off her naked reclining form. In want of a soundtrack for such agreeable debauchery, Sadi put on the Velvet Underground's 'Loaded' whilst Emily searched the room for tantalising accessories. Amongst the host's effects, she found a studded red leather belt and wrapped it lasciviously around her slim waist. Touching her tousled, shoulder length hair, she saw fit to ask, "Do you think I'm pretty...? My face...?" The context was rather poignant and she suddenly seemed a lot younger than her 20 something years.

Unfortunately, hers were not the only insecurities that would scupper a potentially enjoyable evening. Suffering from the familiar shrinkage that afflicts the habitual cocaine user, it soon became woefully apparent that Sadi was in no fit state to engage in the manly act of copulation. "Usually it's as long as his," he insisted - with reference to his limp, shrivelled organ - before declaring that there were no condoms on the premises. He was almost certainly lying but a fiercely competitive nature would never have allowed him to graciously concede. If Sadi couldn't have sex then nobody was having sex. Not in his apartment, at least.

The next 6 hours became a monument to frivolous chatter and sexual frustration. At one point, Sadi suggested his appendage might rise to the occasion if he were allowed a little time alone with our mutual concubine. "Knock yourself out," I said, getting up off the bed and electing to shadow box naked in a far corner of the room. Alas, it was to no avail. "I CAN'T do it with you 'fist fighting' in the background." he moaned. This wasn't Rock N' Roll, it was pure farce and my patience was beginning to wane faster than his dormant love muscle.

At around 6.30am, he suddenly announced, "You guys have to leave now. My mother will be getting up soon." Then he turned to Emily and said, "Well, actually, YOU could stay." I began to get dressed in readiness to leave as Emily scrambled out of bed and searched for her clothes, saying, "Wait…! I'm coming with you…" Presumably, she was inclined to back the horse she might still get a ride on, despite Sadi's protests. When we hit the street and walked back towards the 3 Ducks, I asked her where we could go in order to finish what we had started. "Well, I really like this 2 on 1 thing," she replied. "Do you think Allan might join us…?"

I was aware that she and Allan had 'previous' dating back to her first night in Paris but asking if he fancied a threesome at 7am in the morning didn't seem any less absurd on that basis. Arriving at the hostel to find Allan sipping his morning coffee at end of a 12 hour shift, I relayed Emily's indecent proposal. It would have been difficult for him to refuse without coming across a 'stick in the mud' in light of his gigolo reputation. He tossed me the keys to his shared apartment, saying, "I'll be there in half an hour. Start without me."

Soon, the three of us were assembled in Allan's bedroom and, to my casual relief, he had no issues regarding potency. Alternating between her two willing steeds, Emily had styled her hair in pigtails and was sucking on a lollipop which gave her a teenage cheerleader appearance that she must have found fetching. Daylight penetrated the crème curtains, adding a surreality to the scene as I sensed the encroaching comedown from the night's excesses. I needed a drink. Having satisfied himself in the short term, Allan agreed to go on a beer run, leaving me to hold the fort. I had been 'on the boil' for so long at Sadi's place that I was beginning to flag but remained strangely obsessed with maintaining my performance as Emily sat astride me and gyrated.

When Allan returned, 20 minutes later, he had 6 bottled beers under his right arm and some skis that he claimed to have found in the street under his left. At that moment, I caught a detached glimpse of what my life had become: Straddled by a naked Canadian girl sucking a lollipop while my wingman stood in the doorway, clutching a 6 pack of Grimbergen and a pair of fucking Snowblades at half past 8 in the morning.

I had to get out of Paris, before it consumed me.

16/ INSTANT-KARMA

Before the summer was out, Jenny came back across the channel to join me once more. We were happy to see one another again but, inevitably, our issues hadn't simply gone away. Aside from the residual guilt of my philandering, there was the inexorable fact that I was unwilling to relinquish this new persona. I was addicted to attention, ego validation and shallow sexual encounters, particularly with American girls of low intelligence. I was still in residence at 'Chez Sadi' where the regular madness reigned, despite the steadying influence of a woman. Several weeks before the abortive threesome, Sadi had lost that particular presence in his own life when his long term girlfriend left for her native Denmark with no plans to return anytime soon. It affected him very badly and thereafter he sought to anaesthetise himself with alcohol and drugs from dawn to dusk.

6 months shy of my 30th birthday, I was becoming increasingly concerned about the terrible hangovers I was suffering but continued to drink excessively all the same. On the plus side, I had really gone off the coke, following an unpleasant experience after Sadi and I decided to jack it up one night. It was hard to ascertain what had been worse - the sickening rush itself or the precarious trek down the Champs - Elysees on the back of his Vespa in order to purchase the needles. Faithful to my familiar habit of blaming the environment rather than myself, I was keen to leave Paris but there was still the small matter of my unpaid bill at the 3 Ducks to contend with. Matt the barman had said it was a matter of honour and that he would take a dim view if I should leave the city without settling up. Allan and Jason were less sympathetic to their employer and urged me to get on my toes. Since the second opinion was more appealing, Jenny and I got a chunk of money together and caught the Eurostar to Amsterdam. To the best of my knowledge, I am barred from the 3 Ducks Hostel to this day.

In hindsight, we ought to have gone back to the U.K but I was chronically lacking in imagination and seemed determined to retrace the steps that Emma and I had taken several years ago. Upon arrival in 'The Dam', I immediately felt deflated. I thought we might be able to stay with Grietje, to whom I'd been close in Paris, but it soon became obvious that she didn't want me anywhere near her real life. Consequently, we found a hotel near the red light district and rolled up at Rembrandtplein the next morning.

A lot of the old faces were still working the terraces including Richard, Bill, Victor the violinist and Texas Ed. Most of them didn't remember me due to a radically short hair cut I had gotten before leaving France or so I assumed. I struggled to entertain the notion that they had simply forgotten me, irrespective of hairstyle. Although I was a better musician than I had been the first time around with a bigger voice, I quickly grew to hate the daily grind of competing to impress the tourists. At the 3 Ducks, I had been a veritable 'superstar' who only need pluck the opening riff of 'Blister In The Sun' in order to arouse a latter day 'Beatlemania' Here, I was just another street busker and I didn't care for it one bit. Luckily, I would not be required to endure the anonymity for too much longer.

In an effort to save money, we starting camping in a tent given to us by one of the other musicians in the circle. Generally, after a hard day's work, we would pitch it on a campsite on the outskirts of the city but, one particular evening, I suggested that we could avoid costs entirely if we simply found a secluded patch of grass. Bureaucracy meant nothing to me and so Jenny's reservations about spending the night on an expanse of greenery opposite a traffic island fell on deaf ears. At roughly midnight, we were disturbed from our slumbers by a male and female cop duo who informed us that it was illegal to camp on the site in question and respectfully asked us to move on.

Thinking they wouldn't be back before morning, I paid lip service of obedience before motioning Jenny back into the tent and falling asleep. When the same two police officers returned at 5am, they seemed rather annoyed that we had disrespected their authority and told us that we were under arrest. As I churlishly disassembled the tent, I called the male officer a 'motherfucker' under my breath which caused him to make a beeline for me. I was handcuffed behind my back and we were both thrown in the back of a squad car and taken to a Police Station in an area that I didn't recognise. Daylight had broken by the time we arrived and I was in the foulest of moods.

The crux of the matter was that they wanted to fine us 250 Guilders for illegal camping. The problem therein was that we didn't have 250 Guilders and both parties knew full well that they would never see us again if they released us before payment was made. "I'd like to make a deal with you," said the surprisingly pleasant lady desk sergeant. "We let you go now but we keep the guitar until the fine is paid...?" I wasn't aware that we had any leverage for negotiation so I agreed to the 'deal' and we were soon on our way. Since the guitar was integral to my survival in any foreign city, we now needed the equivalent of a 100 pound sterling in order to make any money at all.

Unheroic though it was, I made a reverse charge call to Mum and availed her of our predicament. Not unaccustomed to such incidents involving her first born son, she agreed to wire me enough money to pay the fine and booked us a pair of flights to Liverpool for the next day. 48 hours later we were sat in the dining room of the house that she shared with her new husband, Steve, listening to the obligatory speech about how it was surely time to settle down and cease all this gallivanting. As ever, I made the right noises but my heart wasn't in it.

Within a few days we moved into a house share with Steve's son, Kevin, and his girlfriend in the god forsaken district of Blacon and found temporary work in a soap factory. The comedown was almost more than I could bear. In the 15th arrondissement of Paris I had been a feted 'Rock God' and here I was packing bars of soap surrounded by uncultured scousers. Romantically, Jenny and I were dead in the water but neither one of us could bring ourselves to pull the plug. At the same time, neither of us wanted to live in Blacon or work in a factory and so, after one disagreement too many, we resolved to go our separate ways. For her, that meant back to her mother's place in Gloucester whilst I headed to Ed's new flat in South Wimbledon.

It was late on a Friday night when Ed answered the street door and gave me a hug as he ushered me up the stairs. Despite his absence from the story hitherto, we were already close friends, having met back in '97 when he was working at Blade's 'Planet Pop' stall in Richmond Market. At the time he was 17 but his obsession with all things Punk Rock since the age of 10 had inspired him to track Andy down to the Richmond Hill branch of Threshers after a recent Q Magazine interview had revealed that the former star could be found serving customers there during retail hours. While still at school, he had formed the 'Walking Abortions' and was featured on the hip Channel 4 show 'Naked City' when he and his band mates were only 14. In the interim, he had fronted 'The Cherry Stainz', as managed by Blade and Nils Stevenson, before relations turned sour and hopes of indie stardom were thwarted. By the Autumn of '99, he was the drummer in a punk pop 3 piece called 'Product' and shared the flat opposite South Wimbledon tube station with fellow members Dan and Carolyn.

As we caught up in the lounge over a few drinks, he explained that I could sleep in Dan's room for the next few nights since he had yet to get out of hospital after being beaten up by a nightclub doorman whom he had inadvisably harangued. It wasn't an unusual scenario for Dan, who was a talented singer and guitarist but prone to bouts of obnoxiousness, especially when in his cups. As soon as he was discharged a few days later, the 3 of us quickly morphed into a trio of vodka swilling miscreants about town. We went out most nights of the week and even a quiet evening in would involve the collective consumption of 2 bottles of cheap vodka as we sought to deafen the neighbours with our impeccable music taste.

The weekend was all about Camden Town. Typically, we would finish a bottle of spirits at the flat before venturing downtown on the Northern Line at around 8pm. First stop was The Good Mixer on Inverness Street, the Mecca of Indie Rock gentility and sometime haunt of Graham Coxon or the lesser members of 'Menswear.'

At chucking out time it was on to the Monarch (now known as the Barfly) until 2am before winding up at the Marathon Bar where one could get a portion of chips and a can of Stella whilst being serenaded by the amphetamine fuelled rockabilly of 'Johnny Awesome' or the resident Bebop duo.

Although she often stayed at her parents' place in Sevenoaks, Carolyn was far from elated at my presence in the flat. Not unreasonably, she felt that I was impinging on her intimacy with the boys. At the outset, they had been something of a little family in their matching black shirts, pin striped trousers and converse all stars but when things degenerated into an orgy of laddish excess, she would ask precisely how long I intended to stay. At any rate, the cute unisex bass player was hedging her bets with a band called My Vitriol who (ironically) had more commercial potential than Product. When said band duly signed to Infectious Records and she did what any young ambitious musician would have done, she was harshly construed as the rat leaving the sinking ship and became the butt of all jokes. The final straw was the discovery that someone had ejaculated into her industrial sized tub of hair gel during a midweek jollification. When she moved out a few days later assisted by her mother, the latter looked sufficiently po - faced for me to assume that she had been informed of the atrocity. Being innocent of the deed, I merely hoped that she didn't think I was the culprit.

With the new millennium upon us, I quickly inherited Carolyn's room and her position in the band, although I was no bass player in any credible sense. When I arrived on the scene, Ed and Dan both had jobs - at a Wimbledon shoe shop and a Turnham Green tailors, respectively. Under my bad influence, both quit their daytime responsibilities within a few months in order to free up more time for drinking and tomfoolery. And - bad influence though I undoubtedly was - it was usually Dan who started the fights.

Some people like to say that boxing skills mean nothing on the street. This is, of course, abject nonsense. Since getting shorn in

Paris, I had grown my hair and dyed it black thus once again resembling an indie fop who couldn't punch his way through a wall of confetti. Consequently, my fist fighting prowess always came as a shock to the Friday night beer boys that we found ourselves at odds with on a reasonably regular basis. Whether Dan was emboldened by the addition of an ex-boxer to his clique or was simply being his disagreeable self was unclear but altercations came thick and fast. In fairness, he wasn't always to blame: One night we brawled with a gang of four who tried to attack our 'manager' in the Dublin Castle and, on another occasion, I had a stand up outside Limelight Nightclub on Shaftesbury Avenue with a tall black guy who had cast aspersions on our heterosexuality. Such incidents were always regarded as a victory of some sort and further evidence of our Rock N' Roll credentials.

We played 2 gigs as the new incarnation of Product before our camaraderie was blown to smithereens. Foolishly, Jenny and I decided to give things another go and so she came back to London and moved into the flat on Kingston Road. Rather inconveniently, it was located above the letting agents who were responsible for the property which made it increasingly difficult to ignore their constantly annoying demands for rent. The police had been called on more than one occasion due to our ribaldry and when Ed hurled an empty bottle of rum through the window by way of a crescendo for his naked rendition of 'TV Eye' on a Tuesday lunchtime, a voice from the bathroom supply store below was heard to cry, "YOU LOT HAVE GONE TOO FAR THIS TIME…!"

Enough was enough as far as the landlord was concerned and we were given notice for the end of June. Strategically, we evacuated on a Sunday when the office was shut so they wouldn't see us leaving with unpaid arrears. Ed moved in to his step mother's pad in Norbiton and Dan found a tiny room in Richmond whilst Jenny and I holed up with a friend called Lisa who lived in Morden. But the end was nigh and it would be far more brutal than it need have been had I just left the past where it belonged.

Dan and I were busking one sunny afternoon on the regular District Line route and Jenny had come along for the ride. Desiring to relieve herself but finding the ladies' toilets at Kew Gardens station closed, she opted to use the Gents. A few minutes later she came out complaining that a man therein had exposed himself to her and used coarse language. The offending personage was a 'fat fucker' she explained in a state of indignation. Expecting a short fat white man, I waited for the malefactor only to see a 240 pound black man emerge from the otherwise vacant facilities. Admittedly, he was slightly over his ideal weight but looked more than a handful all the same.

"WHAT did you say to her...?" I asked him.

"She's a nasty hooker, mate, trust me," he replied with a malevolent smirk.

Being so ludicrously confrontational, he was obviously drawing a line and daring me to cross it but I remained hesitant on account of his sheer bulk.

"You need to get yourself some manners," I told him, still sizing up my potential adversary.

"Oh yeah...? So what are you going to do about it...?"

Suddenly Dan thrust an outstretched palm into the man's chest and commanded, "Calm down, mate..!" It was all the excuse our friend needed to lash out and punch Dan in the face as he shouted, "Don't fucking touch me...!" I hit him with a 1-2 and applied a choke hold as his knees dipped, providing an intimate escort to the floor. As I squeezed his fat neck, blood from his nose dripped onto the platform, seemingly in direct correlation. When a pair of London Transport employees with whom I was quite friendly asked me to let him go, I did so, only for the fight to resume as soon as he had regained his feet. Despite his imposing appearance, the guy was actually pretty useless and, after a few more smacks in the mouth, he was persuaded to board the next eastbound train, despite swearing terrible vengeance.

The aftermath should have been celebratory but there was something in the way Dan had reacted to Jenny being slighted, coupled with her indifference to my chivalry, that opened a can of worms. The two of them seemed to have an intimacy that I hadn't noticed before. A few nights later, I confronted Jenny with my suspicions and we had a terrible row whilst Lisa slept in the next room. That night, I had a dream in which we were arguing violently on a vintage London Bus when she suddenly fell from the rear platform and receded into the distance. When I woke up the next morning, she had already gone.

It was several hours later when she called Lisa's landline and calmly informed me:

"I'm breaking up with you and moving in with Dan…"

17/ L.A WOMAN

Entitled or not, I was utterly devastated by their mutual treachery. I could handle losing Jenny, since we were on our last legs but, with the unforeseen soap operatic twist, I had lost my world into the bargain. A world that was risibly paper thin and based on fantasy. I must have assumed that Punk Rock Utopia above a Wimbledon bath store would last forever and we 3 musketeers would never be torn apart. Yet here I was, 30 years old, with nothing to show for the duration besides an acoustic guitar and a drink problem. Worst of all was knowing that I didn't have a leg to stand on, in terms of grievance. I couldn't possibly blame Jenny after all I had put her through and while it was easy to cast Dan as the villain of the piece, I was hardly without sin in the same regard.

My gut instinct was to head back to Paris and seek to lose myself in a sea of North American groupies. I asked Ed to come with me but - having achieved precious little in the last several months besides drinking the local CostCutter dry - he was not inclined to drop everything in favour of another jaunt designed to plug the gaping hole in my self esteem. Feeling desperately sorry for myself, I paid Deb and Malcolm a visit, who had since gotten married and moved to a big house in Ealing. Much to Deb's understandable chagrin, I had missed their wedding because I was too busy holding court at the 3 Ducks the previous summer. Despite her residual disappointment, she took pity on her cousin and gave me a hundred quid with which to facilitate my latest escape plan. I caught the National Express service to Paris the next day.

As I was persona non grata at the 3 Ducks, I plumped for the Aloha on Rue Borrome, also located in the 15th. The two hostels were actually sister properties but, evidently, the management did not communicate obsessively on the subject of undesirable English musicians with shambolic finances. The plan was perfectly simple: I would entertain the young backpackers and acquire the same lofty status that had been so easily garnered a year before, whilst seeking solace in the company of transient young women. Beyond that, perhaps I might hit it off sufficiently well with one of these floozies that she would invite me to her home city. It all sounded simple enough but I had failed to legislate for the after effects of heartbreak.

Like an alcoholic who imagines his disease can be conquered by migration, I had thought that my feelings of loss and betrayal would evaporate as soon as I hit French soil. Unfortunately, I quickly realised that I felt every bit as wretched in 'Gay Paree' as I had done in the arse end of Morden. It didn't even look like the same city that had seemed so magical and pregnant with possibility at the tail end of the millennium. The charisma that had formerly charmed all and sundry was invisible to me as I moped in the hostel bar, covertly sipping from a plastic cup of uber cheap wine and staring at new female arrivals.

A few nights into my stay, I pulled a blonde chick from Oklahoma who went by the name of Francie and was travelling with her gay best friend as a chaperone. Far from providing a shot in the arm, the encounter almost made me feel worse. I compared her body unfavourably to Jenny's more catwalk model form and was relieved that she was too principled to have full sex on a first date, in such unromantic surroundings. A few nights later, I wound up at the apartment of a kooky French University student who had dropped in to the Aloha for a drink, flanked by two friends, and invited to me to a party being hosted a few blocks away. Anne had no such qualms about sex on a first date but I simply couldn't oblige her when it came to the moment of truth. I blamed the drink and gave her that hackneyed speech about having too much respect for her.

I was beginning to feel as if the trip had been a mistake when salvation appeared in the shape of a chirpy Korean girl from California who proffered her hand one Saturday night and said, "Hi, I'm Linda. Pleased to meet you." It was, she explained, her penultimate night in Paris and since she desired to rid herself of any remaining French currency, the beers were on her. She was 24 and pretty in a wholesome way that didn't require an excess of make up or regalia.

Introductions made, we sat at a table near the stairway and shared multiple rounds of Heineken as we talked about our lives and what had brought us to this point. I told her about the fatal body blow that Jenny and Dan had conspired to deal me and she brought me up to speed with a film director in Los Angeles with whom she was continually 'on and off.' As the conversation flowed, she showed me her tattoos: a Celtic design at the bass of her back (latterly known as the 'tramp stamp') and the name of a friend gone too soon engraved on her lower abdomen. Linda was a conceptual artist on the cusp of her 6th year at UCLA and the longer we conversed, the more I was attracted to her. At 2am, the French barman called time and so we said goodnight and retired to our respective dorms. I was smitten and no mistake.

The next morning, I kept an eye out for my new Oriental crush but there was no sign of her at breakfast. At 11am, the hostel having emptied as the assorted international residents embarked on their various tours of the city, I asked the Irish kid on reception if he knew what dorm Linda might be in. He checked the list of reservations and placed a call up to Room 16. Linda answered. She had somehow locked herself in the room and had been trying in vain to escape its confines for the last 20 minutes. Concluding that I had a vested interest, the young lad gave me the key, thus allowing me to play Sir Galahad to her damsel in distress.

I climbed the stairs and opened the door, inviting her surprise that it should be me who had come to the rescue. "You look nice today," she said immediately. For the reader's benefit, I was wearing dark pin striped trousers and a black shirt emblazoned with a dragon emblem. She was clad in turquoise slacks and a white 'wife beater' vest that accentuated her honey coloured skin. "Not as delectable as you," I replied. "What are you up to today....?"

"I don't know... Wanna' do something...?

"How about a trip to the Pompidou Centre...?"

"Ok, let's go," she agreed.

Since Linda had expressed an interest in seeing me do my thing on the Metro, I played a couple of songs and collected a few Francs as we headed to Rambeautu on line 12. Just as I was thinking how dreadfully convenient it was that I could ply my trade and impress my date simultaneously, the RATP pulled us off the train at Gare Montparnasse and began to make grave sounding noises in their mother tongue. The 'Rat Police' as I called them were by far the worst authority I had come across on my travels and routinely treated buskers as if they were drug smuggling paedophiles. Frequently they would accuse me of playing dumb whilst being perfectly fluent in French and trying to convince them otherwise was practically impossible. Linda looked a little worried as the chief 'rat' delivered a drawn out soliloquy that neither of us understood but the upshot was another meaningless penalty notice, signed in triplicate. Maybe the bureaucrat bastard didn't realise that there was more likelihood of him winning the Miss Black America pageant than of me paying the fine that had just been levied. Having been ordered to exit the station, we waited 5 minutes before re - entering and continuing on our way.

The Centre Pompidou is one of Paris' bohemian enclaves devoted to street art, music and mime. As we walked in the Sunday afternoon sunshine taking in the sights and getting to know each other better, I suggested it was time for a beer. I found a small shop that only seemed to stock a super strength brand of lager called 'Amsterdam' and so I purchased two of those. It was 10.6 by Volume and Linda gagged a little as her lips met with its treacle like consistency but she was game and that was important. This wasn't some chintzy little sorority princess I was dealing with. The cans were drained, inhibitions were removed and we started making out by a statue as it began to precipitate ever so softly. An African guy whom I had allowed to play my guitar provided a lilting reggae soundtrack as we kissed and caressed in the rain. Taking temporary leave from our amorous clinch, she asked, "Wanna split another Amsterdam...?"

We headed back to the hostel for early evening and had a few more drinks in the bar before bundling up the stairs and into room 16 with the intention of fully consummating our fledgling passion. Initially, we found the dormitory devoid of occupants as I took off her clothes but no sooner were we ensconced between the sheets of the lower bunk bed than a surfeit of Asian males entered the room, apparently about to turn in for the night. I could scarcely believe that anyone would book into a youth hostel and go to sleep at 8pm but we were far too inebriated not to finish what we had started. I would later learn that Linda had a penchant for slow sex which seemed just as well as we copulated as quietly as possible, against a backdrop of foreign chatter. The whole scene was probably more graphic and inappropriate than we could appreciate in our collectively sozzled state but, eventually, we decided to get up and go for a walk in the moonlight before returning at a more regular adult bedtime.

The next thing I knew, it was morning and she was standing at the side of the bed, fully clothed with a large rucksack attached, preparing to head for Charles De Gaulle and back to L.A. Perhaps embarrassed by what had transpired the night before, she muttered, "Erm.. Bye..." and walked towards the door. "Wait a second," I said, remaining horizontal. "Do you have an email address...?" She opened a side pocket and tossed me a small scrap of paper on which had been scrawled 'lsk@UCLA.edu'. And with that, she was gone.

I stayed in Paris for another week before returning to London in appreciably better spirits than I had left. Like any hopeless romantic, I fancied that I was in love and was suddenly fixated with the idea of the trip to Los Angeles, not that I had an invitation at this stage. After getting into Victoria, I rolled up at Deb and Malcolm's on a Saturday afternoon and was shocked to hear that they were splitting up. I had always viewed them as the perfect middle class couple although there had been tensions since they tied the knot. The atmosphere was extremely subdued and Deb left the next day although she wouldn't say where she was going. Suddenly alone in a 4 bed roomed house, Malcolm said I may as well take the attic room until I had figured out my next move. Looking back, moving in with Deb's ex-husband to be probably wasn't the most sensitive or loyal thing for a family member to do but such things were lost on me at the time.

I emailed Linda and she emailed back, leading to further correspondence and a couple of transatlantic telephone calls. I half invited myself, saying that I was planning a trip to the West Coast and wondered if she might be agreeable to a houseguest. She made the right noises while stressing that she lived in Palos Verdes, almost 30 miles from LA, but was expecting to move to an apartment in Hollywood in the next several weeks. We loosely agreed on November for my arrival.

Being as it was early September, I had some work to do if the dream was become a reality. By now, Ed was working in a call centre on Richmond Hill and - breaking the habit of almost a decade - I decided to follow his lead. The job involved interviewing various respondents for a slew of market research surveys and collating their responses on a computer. Although the subject matter was almost always mind numbingly inane, I actually quite enjoyed it. I didn't mind talking to secretaries, I.T managers or company directors about whatever it might be and there was good banter to be had on the floor. I got to sit next to my best mate, going for lunchtime pints, and there were always scores of hot young ladies in the office of a varied international flavour. It was another example of mainstream life not being as horrible as I'd imagined.

With an extreme sense of mission, I frequently put in 12 hour shifts in order to save enough cash for my trip to the City of Angels. It wasn't so much about chasing tail as chasing a dream and a vision although - in the pre social media era - I could scarcely remember what she looked like. Even Malcolm was impressed with my single mindedness despite the predictable battering his drinks cabinet sustained during my tenure. In October, I got a message from Linda announcing that she had procured a place in West Hollywood and everything was set for my reception. The tone of her emails was friendly but not flirtatious and I had no idea if I was on a promise or the one night stand in Paris would prove to be precisely that.

At the weekend, I would do a bit busking so as not to touch my savings. On one such Saturday, I was seated on a bench at Southfields station, counting the money when a heavy set black guy sat next to me suddenly asked, "Excuse me... Have I seen you before...?" I looked up from my bag of coins and realised that I was face to face with the same clown I'd had a ruck with several weeks earlier at Kew Gardens. I fleetingly thought about acting tough before I heard myself saying: "I'm not aware that we are previously acquainted, sir."

He eyed me sceptically but said, "Ok.. Sorry, mate. No problem."

Perhaps he considered it a moral victory but I was damned if I was going to defend Jenny's honour a second time.

18/ HOLLYWOOD

After a fitting send off in Camden Town with Ed and mutual friends, I flew from Heathrow to LAX on Thursday November 2, 2000. The flight took 11 hours - the longest I had yet endured - and I drank whisky and cokes just as fast as the BA girls could serve them throughout. Nonetheless, I felt stone cold sober when I got through immigration and Linda was waiting for me at the gate at around 4pm local time. She looked as cute as I remembered and gave me a hug before we headed towards the car park to retrieve her SUV truck. Cruising down West Century Boulevard, I gazed at the endless procession of vehicles and palm trees in the warm California sun and felt agreeably far from Ealing's dismal grey skies. With her permission, I shoved a carefully complied mix tape into the stereo, thus declaring the adventure in official commencement.

Following 10 minutes of small talk, she cut to the chase. "So, anyhow... I've kinda' been seeing Jordan again. The guy I told you about in Paris. And he made me promise that we won't sleep in the same bed together."

"Does he know what happened in Paris...?" I wondered.

"Of course not," she replied.

As disappointing as it might have been, the buoyancy of my mood was hardly affected by her revelation. It seemed safe to assume there would be other Californian girls of exotic lineage and I wasn't convinced that Linda would make good on her promise to whatshisname, regardless. We had only known each other for 36 hours in real time so I could hardly expect her to throw herself at me as soon as I stepped off the plane. I was a romantic but also a pragmatist and remained optimistic as the Small Faces provided a reassuring soundtrack:

'PICKED HER UP ON A FRIDAY NIGHT
SHA LA LA LA LEE, YEAH
I KNEW EVERYTHING GONNA' BE ALRIGHT
SHA LA LA LA LEE (YEAH)'

Linda shared the apartment at 7727 Hollywood Boulevard with a girl of the same age called Michelle and we pretty much hated each other on sight. Logistically, she wasn't unattractive but her attitude was as ugly as the dregs of a 19th century Whitechapel whorehouse. In due course, she would come to embody everything I despised about a certain type of vacuous white American female although, irritatingly, she claimed Cuban heritage. More convivial were the gay neighbours, Jody and Brian, to whom I was immediately introduced as Linda's novelty friend from England. They were long-time buddies from St. Louis, as opposed to a couple, with Brian being the obligatory pantomime dame of the two.

It was a 2 bed roomed property and so - unsure of where I might be sleeping - I dumped my bag and guitar in Linda's room and went to the bathroom to freshen up. "Looks like it's just you and me tonight," she announced when I reappeared in the lounge. Attempting to drum up a gathering for my first night in Tinsel Town, she had been blown out by everyone, including the venerable Jordan - which didn't strike me as a tragedy. Unburdened by the presence of a suspicious boyfriend, we took a walk to the Whiskey A' Go Go on Sunset Boulevard and caught the last few numbers of a punk/metal combo before going outside for a cigarette.

The California smoking ban was already in effect, predating London and New York by a few years and - although I didn't smoke with any real competence - I had acquired the habit since splitting up with Emma. "It's good to see you again," she said.

"You too," I agreed. "Although we don't really know each other, do we..?"

"Let's just go with it," she suggested.

Coming from one of the most vibrant metropolitan areas in the world, the Sunset Strip seemed almost sedate like an exclusive music biz party. It didn't resemble the cauldron of sex, drugs & rock n' roll that Axl and Slash had reportedly occupied 15 years earlier but that didn't matter. I was getting drunk for the second time in a single day in pleasantly iconic surroundings with the girl of my lyrical dreams. I was well aware that the situation could have been vastly worse.

Growing weary of 3 chord garage band fodder, we moved to a joint up the street from which the strains of Duran Duran's 'Girls On Film' emanated as we entered. I ordered the drinks and as I stepped away from the bar she leaned in and kissed me on the mouth. In mock protest, I admonished her:

"I thought we weren't supposed to be doing this, honey…?" in need of a leak, I disengaged and told her, "I'll be back in a minute."

"Well, I HOPE so," came the response.

Linda's monogamous constraints were all but forgotten when I returned from 'the John' and the bar crawl continued, punctuated with acceptable foreplay within the boundaries of public decency. We finished up at a place called 'Miyagi's' where one could eat sushi and sing karaoke in the midst of aspiring actors and musicians on the cusp of elusive fame. As we ambled up the hill towards Hollywood Boulevard at around 1am, a faint chill in the air served as license to remain closely huddled. "You gonna' do the Disneyland thing, Ben…?" she teased. It had been a difficult few months but I had survived the misery of my rejection and landed on my feet again. I felt as if Disneyland had come to me.

Back at the pad, a man was seated on the porch - apparently in vigil - and I instinctively thought it might be her boyfriend. "Oh no, that's not him..!" I was quickly reassured. After going to the bathroom to brush her teeth, she suddenly appeared in the bedroom wearing only white briefs and a short silk white pyjama top that more than half revealed her caramel tits. "Sadly, we have to sleep together," she decreed, "Because I only have one bed." We curled up in that fashion that women call 'spoons' but she was unresponsive when I placed a hand on her right breast. Linda probably figured she'd been unfaithful enough for one day. Having been awake for more than 24 hours, I had no trouble nodding off.

The next morning, the lovely Michelle stuck her head around the door to inform us that Jordan had turned up at midnight asking where Linda was and generally 'acting like a crazy, jealous boyfriend.'
Another man might have had ripples of concern that he had stumbled into a potentially incendiary situation but I wasn't bothered. Looking back I had impressive reserves of chutzpah, perhaps bordering on plain cheek. Linda left the apartment to go to class and Michelle, attempting to be civil, advised me of a few tourist attractions in proximity.

Since Mann's Chinese Theatre and the Walk Of Fame held zero appeal, I went back to The Strip and found an Irish Bar called 'Dublin's' for the purpose of a 'livener.' I downed a couple of pints in lieu of lunch and then made my way down Santa Monica Boulevard to Melrose Avenue. Much of Hollywood was eerily quiet compared to London but Melrose seemed a little more happening, populated as it was by a mixture of hipsters, vagrants and aspiring fashion models. I was especially enamoured to see one punk couture shop displaying Eater T - Shirts in the window and wondered if Blade knew that his image was being flogged in such a far flung location. In the modern era I'd have taken a photo and tagged him but at the turn of the millennium one simply committed such things to memory.

Later that evening, Linda and I had dinner in a Korea Town restaurant with a few of her friends from college. Jordan was scheduled to attend but had stormed off in protest after arguing with her outside the apartment, insisting that a man ought to have the undivided attention of his lady on a Friday night. I couldn't really blame him for having misgivings about the arrangement. I was sharing a bed with his girlfriend, when all said and done. Not long after we finished eating, the jet lag caught up with me, resulting in a swift drive back to Hollywood Boulevard and an early night. Linda was tired, too, and so we curled up together once more in platonic purgatory.

The following night, I got to meet my love rival and found him to be urbane and affable. Jordan wasn't stupid and obviously understood the threat that I represented but chose to play it cool, turning on the charm. "I'm sorry about storming off last night, bro, but this is a difficult situation, you know what I mean…?" I knew exactly what he meant. He was 29 but looked a little older with dark hair and a close cropped beard. He had the air of a man who could handle himself, if push came to shove, but seemed too cultured to fight over a woman. After cocktails in the yard, we drove to his apartment which I can only describe as being somewhere else in L.A. I couldn't get a feel for the topography of a city that looked the same everywhere you went, with its limitless intersecting roads, palm trees, bungalows, hot dog stands and restaurants.

The three of us watched a classic blaxploitation cartoon called 'Heavy Traffic' before Linda and Jordan retired to bed, leaving me on the sofa watching HBO. It felt a little weird to know that the object of one's desires might be getting violated down the hallway but such feelings were perfectly manageable at this early stage. The next morning, after breakfast, Linda and I set off to Venice Beach for a Sunday stroll, "There'll be a mob there today," warned Jordan, "But you guys have a good day." His fears seemed to have been allayed now that the ice was broken. The formerly mysterious British invader was an ok guy, he had evidently surmised.

Despite Jordan's prediction, Venice wasn't rammed in the first week of November. We took a long walk across the sands, encountering tourists, buskers and skaters in tolerable numbers, linking hands before long and generally behaving like lovers entwined. At one point, a black guy in a Rasta style hat with a target design electric guitar came flying down the boardwalk on land-rollers, cranking out distorted heavy metal riffs as he went. He was, Linda said, the Patron Saint of Venice Beach and had been featured on TV. By the time we stopped for calamari at a conveniently situated beachside restaurant, I was firmly besotted with her. She scarcely wore anything besides jeans and a wife beater but an addictive air of femininity juxtaposed with bubblegum American cuteness had cast a spell. Furthermore, I knew she was feeling it, too. Jordan seemed like a nice guy but, frankly, he was in my way.

We were still trudging alongside the waves when the sun went down at 6pm. As we missed our turning, she confessed, "I did it deliberately 'cos I wanted to walk for longer with you." It was one of those idyllic moments that one might happily have prolonged forever but, unfortunately, she was due at her parents' house in Pomona for dinner. Consequently, she dropped me back at the pad before embarking on the 40 minute journey to a place I had only ever heard of in relation to 'Sugar' Shane Mosley. On that basis alone it seemed worth a visit but the likelihood of an invitation was apparently not great. By her own testimony, Linda's old man was a fiercely puritanical clergyman who had once said that the only women who enjoyed sex were prostitutes and sluts. Perhaps she thought we wouldn't get along.

By the middle of the following week, our simmering lust was allowed to express itself after a raucously drunken night in a mocked up English theme pub on Sunset called 'Ye Olde Coach And Horses.' The morning after, Linda skipped class and drove us back to Venice Beach for a heart to heart, picking up Taco Bell en route. As I chomped on a burrito supreme she said, "I think I've put us in a fucked up situation." My side of the equation was simple: I wanted her and could scarcely see further than the end of my nose at the best of times. Being female, she probably had a whole host of concerns relating to that mythical realm known as 'The Future.' With no work visa and a woefully limited budget, I was almost certainly passing through - unless she felt like marrying me. Perhaps the financially stable movie director with his all important American birthright might yet prove the better bet. Before the conversation became too intense - and at variance with L.A autumn protocol- I took a dip in the sea. I tried to coax her into joining me but, ultimately, she declined to swim in her underwear.

For the next 10 days or so, Linda's stance chopped and changed as she struggled to make definite judgements concerning her love life. Tired of second guessing her emotions, coupled with pressure from Michelle to vacate the apartment, I decided on a sabbatical to San Diego. I stayed for a few days on campus at the USD with an 18 year old chick called Heather, whom I had also met on the last Parisian excursion. Our association was purely platonic and I only had eyes for Linda, in any case. As friendly as they were, I didn't find her freshman peer group overly stimulating and soon found myself in the university library, typing what amounted to a confessional love letter to 'my honey coloured vision of bliss.'

My honey coloured vision of bliss responded affirmatively and so I caught a train back to L.A on a Friday afternoon. On the Saturday, we got into the truck and drove from Sunset Boulevard to the Circus Circus Hotel Casino in Las Vegas, retracing the steps of Hunter S. Thompson and his 'attorney' in the genre defining novel. Since my entire world was predicated on the maintenance of a carefully constructed fantasy, the attention to detail was vital. At some point in the middle of a 5 hour journey through mostly faceless desert, Jordan called Linda's cell phone. "I'm going to Vegas for the weekend, I'll talk to you when I get back," she told him, refusing to elaborate.

Eventually, we arrived on The Strip and checked into our predictably massive double room containing 2 king-size beds. Following a swift change of clothes, we hit the casino floor without further ado in search of a civilised beverage. At this point in my life, I was pretty much either hung over or drunk and rebounded exclusively between the two opposing states. The commendable thing about Vegas was that one could drink absolutely anywhere. An absurdly garish cocktail in a 4 foot long receptacle could be purchased from one particular bar and transported through the lobby of a neighbouring establishment without anyone batting an eyelid. Or else you could simply walk into a casino swigging your own liquor straight from the bottle. Considering that much of America confined its more impulsive drinkers to the subterfuge of a brown paper bag, it seemed like a major selling point to me.

The sheer sensory overload of Sin City is intoxicating to all but the most groin dead. The Mirage, Treasure Island, The Luxor, The Venetian and New York, New York. Given the genealogy of our romance, The Paris - with its smaller facsimile of the Eiffel Tower - held a special resonance but the neon majesty of the MGM Grand and a 13 dollar buffet that would have made Caligula's banquets look like a prison punishment diet took precedence. As we sat down to a ludicrous excess of high end cuisine, Linda voiced her modest proposal: "Erm… I don't know how you feel but, since we're in Vegas, I kinda' feel like seeing some naked chicks. Can we go to a strip bar..?"

It would have been churlish to have vetoed her wishes and so I merely insisted that we go to Caesar's Palace first in order that I could shadow box on the hallowed ground where the 'Fab Four' had contested their legendary dust ups.

The next few hours were killed hopping from one casino to another, watching the show bands, high rollers and pristine hookers who loomed large in the jigsaw of endless characters in a perpetual human drama. In accordance with her ladyship's whims, our last stop was a 24 hour strip joint known as 'Cheetah's on Western Avenue. It was a far cry from the Soho clip joints, with a gamut of elite level pussy in the United Colours of Benetton, all vying for attention and gratuities. After 90 minutes of titillation and tequila, Linda said, "Let's go back to the hotel and have some fun."

We caught a the cab back to Circus Circus and she asked the driver if he could score any coke. "Usually I can but it's too late now," he replied apologetically. It was 3am when he dropped us outside the lobby and we made our way into the lift. Any expectations that Vegas sex would outrank Hollywood sex were dampened as we got our groove on but the once before falling asleep. No doubt it would have been different had the cabbie's drug connections been more nocturnally minded.

I awoke 6 hours later with the grandmother of all hangovers, staring out of the window at Vegas' lurid daytime alter ego. Like the loose woman picked up in a bar after midnight, suddenly denuded of jewellery and make up, it didn't look anywhere near as beguiling as it had done the night before. I needed a beer and something to eat, in that order. We got ourselves together and I grabbed a 6 pack of Desperados and a burger that I ate in the truck as we began the long journey back to L.A. When we got there, Linda told Jordan that she and I were an item. He was terribly civilised about the whole thing, driving over the next night with a few of her belongings and a poignant mix tape. He even shook her hand before getting on his way, which I found almost comically dignified. Had the boot been on the other foot, it's highly unlikely I'd have taken it with the same aplomb.

19/ GRAND THEFT AUTO

Shortly after getting back from Vegas, Linda and I went to a gay club one night with Jody and Yuri, who shared the apartment upstairs with a guy from New York called Messiah. Ordinarily, the 6 of us hung out but Messiah must have been otherwise engaged and Brian was having an early night ahead of a trip back home to St. Louis in the morning. Half an hour before the club closed, Jody met a redneck drug dealer in the car park who was pushing crystal meth and invited him and his sidekick back to the ranch for what amounted to an all night bender. The moustachioed redneck went by the name of Geoff and probably hailed from some outpost in Wyoming but I didn't catch his accomplice's name with whom I nearly came to blows after he made a pass at Linda that was neither subtle nor appropriate. An altercation was averted and everyone got into snorting lines of 'glass' which was like speed but came on quicker and smoother.

At 7.30 am, Brian suddenly entered the lounge and was aghast to discover that Jody had allowed two such unsavoury looking strangers into the sanctity of their home. In a fit of pique, he read the riot act, insisting that the drug peddling pair of Jerry Springer rejects left immediately and never darkened the threshold again. He further expressed his disappointment that Linda and I would be a party to such tawdry antics before exiting in a petulant funk and taking a taxi to the airport.

Linda had a gay and lesbian literature class to attend at 9am and suggested it would be fun if I came along. "Can we do that...?" I asked. "It's a big class and nobody will notice an extra person," she reckoned. We got into the truck, grabbing a couple of coffees on the way which immediately reignited the crystal meth. As we turned off Laurel Avenue, huge inflatable Dalmatians hung over the Sunset Strip by way of a promotion for the upcoming film 'Rugrats In Paris.' I was still teeth grindingly high and painfully in love with the girl at the wheel as the outsize speckled canines bobbed in the sky, apparently in sync with Jefferson Airplane's 'Don't You Want Somebody To Love.' It was, I concluded, the stuff that dreams were made of.

We arrived at Linda's class slightly late and took a seat together near the front of the room. A bald, black professor expounded on the hidden gay meanings of Tennessee Williams' 'A Streetcar Named Desire' while I listened intently. When he at last invited comments, I immediately piped up, claiming that the central theme running through the entire story was one of lost innocence. I had neither read the play nor seen the screen adaption but spoke with the authority of a man who might actually have written it. At that moment it occurred to me that anybody could 'steal' an American college education provided they did not require accreditation at the end of it.

The lecture concluded and we drove to the beach where I waxed lyrical for hours, so inspired and reinvented did I feel now that I had been to 'University.' Back at Linda's gaff, I drank neat gin in an effort to override the inevitable comedown. Any committed amphetamine head will tell you that the last phase of a binge is characterised by a visceral horniness that can only be sated by dirty animal sex or furious onanism. Consequently. I was rather disappointed to learn that Linda was not in the mood for relations that night.

A few days later, I went over to Jody and Brian's on a Sunday afternoon and saw Geoff seated on the couch like a bad penny. Brian was still in Missouri and Jody had clearly gone against his wishes, presumably in want of more drugs. With apparently zero sense of protocol, Geoff made uncouth enquiries about the nature of my relationship with Linda, suggesting that we might have a threesome if it wasn't altogether serious between us. And if she was into pussy, he added, then he could always get his girlfriend in on the act. "This is Hollywood, bro," he said, as if that geographical fact somehow excused his abject lack of refinement. Feeling as if my day would be vastly improved by his removal from my field of vision, I made my excuses and went back to Linda's.

It was 48 hours later when Jody knocked on the door in his hospital work clothes with an air of desperation in his voice. "Have you seen, Geoff..?" he asked. "Not since Sunday afternoon," I admitted. "Why...?"

"BRIAN'S CAR IS MISSING...!" he replied, allowing a moment for the terrifying implications of that news to sink in. Never the sharpest tool in the box, Jody had made the astonishingly rookie mistake of leaving Geoff in the apartment while he went to work. Not one to look a gift horse in the mouth, Geoff had taken the keys to the resident's car park and driven off in Brian's red Corvette Stingray. The car was his pride and joy and might have cost in excess of thirty thousand dollars. Explaining that it had been 'half inched' by the same dodgy, despicable bastard he had barred from the house merely days before was going to prove extremely awkward. Particularly since Brian was due home that same evening.

Perhaps hoping that it could be resolved before his plane touched down, Jody asked Linda and me to report the theft to the Los Angeles County Sheriff at West Hollywood Station. When we got there, a jovial black cop on reception seemed rather sceptical about the whole saga.

"So, it's not your car...?"

"No," we conceded.

"So who is the victim..?"

"Well, we'd rather not say as he doesn't know about it yet."

"So how do you know the car has been stolen..?"

"Erm.. because it's not there anymore..."

Grinning broadly, he advised, "Guys, I think you need to get your story together and come back tomorrow."

Jody bit the bullet and called Brian's cell phone when he got into LAX at around 6pm. Brian, upon hearing what had transpired, issued a hail of expletives before hanging up. Afraid to face his roommate alone, Jody requested that Linda and I stay with him for moral support. The air hung heavy as we waited for the inevitable confrontation and wondered if their domestic harmony might be permanently compromised by such an unconscionable fuck up. In due course, Brian flounced through the door, clad in a leather suit with a large hold-all slung over his shoulder. It was clear he was in no mood for company and hadn't expected Linda and me to be present. With nobody knowing quite what to say, the silence was suddenly broken by a TV commercial for an upcoming stoner comedy with the hilariously apposite title of 'DUDE, WHERE'S MY CAR....?"

Any hilarity, of course, was best appreciated if you didn't happen to be the recent owner of a 2 door luxury sports car that would soon be found abandoned in New Mexico, looking more worse for wear than a suicide bomber's genitals.

But I hear that Brian got over it, eventually.

20/ ARYANS AND ABSINTHE

My California dream went downhill after I struck out at the Banana Bungalow. Although things were going well with Linda, Michelle was making it increasingly uncomfortable for me to stay in the apartment and would constantly ask about my 'plans.' As a result, it seemed imperative that I find a job and my own accommodation if I was to stay in L.A for much longer. On that vague premise, I was wandering aimlessly in the Hollywood Hills one afternoon when I stumbled on the youth hostel of the aforementioned name. I went inside and was encouraged to find a young English lad called Dave working on reception. I asked if there might be any vacancies. He disappeared momentarily and returned with the manageress. As luck would have it, they were looking to recruit someone and I was asked to fill out a form before beginning a week's trial the next day. I professed to have papers and figured I could wing it, just as I had done in Denver ten years earlier.

As much as I got a kick out of answering the phone and saying, "Hello, Banana Bungalow Hollywood, this is Ben speaking, how may I help you?" it became obvious after 3 days that the blag wasn't going to work. The company ran a tight ship and if you couldn't provide proof of a social security number then they didn't employ you. After a Saturday night keg party, I didn't bother going back although I probably drank enough free beer to break even on my labour. It was a shame since, had I got through the trial, I could have lived on the premises. Out of funds, with Michelle's microscopic reserves of goodwill long since exhausted, I flew back to London in mid December.

Good old Malcolm extended his hospitality at Croft Gardens once more and I settled back into work at the call centre. He seemed to regard me as his errant kid brother despite the diametrically opposite nature of our lives. Still clinging to my exotic Hollywood fantasies, by February 2001 I was seeing a 20 year old German heiress who spoke 6 languages but was - in other ways - as daft as a brush. Her name was Carina and she worked part time at the call centre whilst studying for a role in corporate finance at the

University College School in Hampstead. Aesthetically, she was attractive, with long brown locks and a flawlessly lithe figure but, being more Covent Garden than Camden Town, she simply wasn't my type.

One day in March, after a typically excessive night on the piss, Ed and I bunked off work and headed to Soho in search of diversion. For some reason he seemed inordinately keen that we should procure some absinthe and go to the HMV store in Piccadilly. Exercising laudable caution, we limited ourselves to 20 centilitre bottles of the lethal Swiss spirit, purchased incrementally from 'Gerry's Wines' on Old Compton Street. After the third bottle, my last recollection was of a harmless exchange with a pair of street hookers before coming to in the back of a riot van, being struck repeatedly on the thigh with what felt like a truncheon.

As 4 or 5 coppers dragged us through the custody suite at Chandos Place nick, I could see that Ed was in a terrible state, his vacant eyes peering through a mass of crimson blood. He looked like Henry Cooper at the conclusion of the second Ali fight. "What the fuck have you done to him, you cunts..?" I demanded to know as they slung me in a cell and I immediately passed out for several hours.

"Benjamin, are you sober enough to be released yet...?"

I was, in fact, still rather drunk but stood up and assured the lovely WPC that I was more than ready for another stab at civilian life. I had no idea how much time had elapsed since our arrest or precisely what we had done to get a tug in the first place. As they booked me out and returned my personal effects, it suddenly occurred to me to ask where Ed was. Bizarrely, the desk sergeant could only tell me that my friend was no longer in their custody but had no further information on his whereabouts. Back on the street, I walked down to Trafalgar Square and called Ed's girlfriend, Caroline, from a pay phone:

"Hi Caroline... Do you know where Ed is...?"

"NO...! He was with YOU...! What have you done this time..? WHERE is he...?"

"Well, please don't overreact but the last I saw him, he was covered in blood at the cop shop in Chandos Place. They've let me out but they won't tell me where he is..."

She and Ed were due to catch a Eurostar to Paris, early the next morning with his parents and she was clearly holding me directly responsible for the likelihood that it wasn't going to happen. Since there was no reasoning with the hysterical woman, I refused to waste another 20 pence on the conversation. Next, I dialled Ed's father, Ted, who was far more stoic about the situation and had managed to ascertain that his son was in St. Thomas' Hospital on account of his injuries. I arrived at the emergency department in time to catch the comical sight of Ed - with his spiky, pillar box red hair and sea-foam surgical gown - caressing the lady doctor's cheek in oddly Corinthian fashion. The sudden introduction of a dextrose drip appeared to have made him frisky and unaware of standard protocol. He was discharged after midnight and still made the trip to Paris, albeit looking like a post fight Rocky Balboa and remaining in the doghouse throughout.

The next day, Malcolm opined that we had 'probably deserved a good kicking' but Carina was much more sympathetic and took me away to her obscure German hometown for the weekend to convalesce. I had scarcely been back a week when I got fired from the call centre for back chatting a respondent who had tried to belittle me. I viewed the episode as yet more evidence of my proud, intractable spirit but it was probably fairer to say that my big mouth had impacted negatively on my affairs once again. Not content with making one bad decision, I then agreed to take up residence in a 3 bed roomed house in Streatham to which Ed's dad had a tenuous claim of ownership.

To cut a long story short, Ted, a tabloid journalist, had been sued many years previously by a disgruntled former colleague over the misplacement of some photographs depicting a ferry disaster. He had lost the action and subsequently filed for bankruptcy. Having recently inherited the house when an elderly relative passed away, he was naturally concerned that the asset might fall into the hands of his eternal nemesis. For some reason, he also concluded that such an eventuality could be circumvented by the mere fact of my occupation. Rent free, he hastened to add.

Unfortunately, it turned out to be one of the more ridiculous strategies in legal history and I was turfed out within a fortnight by an unsympathetic estate agent, accompanied by the local rozzers. Now jobless and homeless, I was reduced to staying with Carina at her modest student digs on Finchley Road. I had not treated her well during our dalliance and would constantly berate her for an intrinsic lack of similarity to Linda, to whom I was still emotionally betrothed. At odds with the notion that hell hath no fury like a woman scorned, she made a wonderfully magnanimous gesture.

"You haven't had much luck recently. Would you like to go to America to see Linda..?"

"And how is that going to happen...?"

"Surprise, surprise... I pay for your ticket."

I should have been too proud to accept such generosity from a girl 11 years my junior but my sense of entitlement superseded any latent natural decency. I would venture across the pond once more, I agreed, with her kind sponsorship but suggested that I start the expedition in New York. As nonsensical as it was to any reunion agenda, I figured that I would have a better chance finding work and accommodation in the Big Apple and perhaps Linda might be persuaded to take a trip to the East Coast.

When I flew from Gatwick to JFK on Wednesday April 18, 2001, I had 103 dollars in my pocket.

21/ HARLEM

For the first 2 weeks, I stayed with Luc in Jersey City. A 15 minute PATH ride from Manhattan on the other side of the Hudson River, its location afforded a fine view of the legendary skyline. Since Luc had been an integral part of the 3 Ducks Class of '99, we had stayed in touch and seized the opportunity to renew our acquaintance now that he was enrolled at the Eugene Lang College of Liberal Arts in New York. 2 years ago he had been a carefree, if precocious, 17 year old but already he bore worrying signs of maturation in the time that had since elapsed. Essentially, he appeared to have aspirations beyond drinking, playing guitar and chasing women, which was rather disturbing to an arrested adolescent like myself.

With Luc focused on his studies, I spent a lot of time carousing with his classmates, a few of whom took me to a place called the Roadhouse one night, where I randomly bumped into Ted of Way Waywardson 'fame.' Not having laid eyes on one another since the day he dropped me at Denver airport 11 years ago, it seemed an extraordinary piece of random fate requiring due celebration. He had gained 40 pounds after marrying a girl from Brooklyn and was still playing guitar, although I got the impression he did something else for a living.

In my case, playing guitar seemed the only plausible way of making a living and I soon learned that the New York population were considerably more tolerant of buskers than their English/ French counterparts. A fair percentage of London Underground users saw my ilk as glorified beggars but the average New Yorker evidently admired any man prepared to sing for his supper. Testing the waters on the F - Train between 14th St and Coney Island, I took 60 odd dollars on the first day and breathed a sigh of relief. The benign acceptance of street musicians was also reflected in the attitudes of the NYPD and the Metropolitan Transport Authority. One on particular afternoon, a uniformed cop on the train tossed me 5 bucks shortly before I was asked to serenade the assembled MTA workers in one of the control rooms on the platform. Seemingly, there was not a jobsworth to be found in the entire city.

When my allotted 2 weeks at Luc's came to an end I checked into the Park View Hotel at 110 Central Park North, the official border of Harlem. Despite the area's historical reputation as a no go area for Caucasians, it didn't seem an especially dangerous neighbourhood, although few of the international guests ventured much further than the subway station or the local deli. The hotel was run by an Italian American guy in this mid 30s called Robert and his right hand man - and head of security - was a hulking entity known as 'Big Steve', who looked like Biggie Smalls. It cost 16 dollars a night for a shared room, usually occupied by 3 other people.

When I arrived on a Sunday evening, I immediately familiarised myself with the hardcore group, who effectively lived in the hostel whilst waiting for bigger and better things. There was a contingent of Brits and Europeans with various back stories and a regular flow of Americans who would come to New York with dreams of making it big in whatever industry they imagined themselves to be talented. In the next several weeks I would meet singers, models, comedians and screenwriters who were chewed up and spat out by the harsh realities of the concrete jungle.

My constant roommate for much of the time was a skinny Mancunian alcoholic called Paul who had shunned whatever semblance of a life he had in the U.K and vowed never to return. He was one of those drunks who became loud and abrasive when in his cups but was shy and withdrawn without a drink in him. By day, he worked as a waiter which was an interesting choice of profession for a man who seemed to have the severe DTs every morning. One shuddered to think of him delivering a tray of hot beverages before noon. At some point during my stay he would be ejected for his flagrantly excessive boozing, only to wind up getting his right foot mangled in a collision between two yellow taxis. By the summer, unable to work or claim benefits, he could be seen hobbling around on crutches and sleeping in the park. He must have really pissed somebody off in Manchester was all I could think.

Another character from the North West of England was Mark, a short, stocky 28 year old who worked on reception and fancied himself as a ladies' man. Although he would frequently seek to ingratiate himself with the more attractive female clientele, he constantly alluded to a girlfriend called Claire, who was also from Manchester but allegedly something of an international traveller herself. In time, I would get to know her all too intimately under circumstances that neither he nor I could possibly have predicted.

Having found an affordable place to stay and perfected my gig on the subway, I felt stable enough to give Linda a call and announce my presence on the East Coast. Although I hadn't exactly taken a vow of celibacy, I still thought of her constantly while suspecting that it might not be fully mutual. Whatever the truth, she sounded happy enough to hear from me and said she was planning a trip to New York in June. We could meet up then, it was suggested. In the meantime, there was plenty to keep me occupied; not least the nightly ad hoc parties in the Park View common room. As always, I played heavily on the leverage and 'celebrity' that the guitar afforded me and was seldom short of acolytes who wanted to buy me a drink.

To give myself a break from busking, I got a job with a removals firm called Arthur Werner. For foreigners who didn't have papers, removals seemed to be the industry of choice and most of my colleagues were Black American, Hispanic, Irish or Eastern European. The company was based in the Bronx but the various assignments would take us all over upstate New York and into suburbs of New Jersey and Connecticut. Unfortunately, I didn't get to see a lot of scenery, being frequently obliged to ride in the back of the truck with an obligatory raging hangover. It was back breaking work for an insubstantial wage but the tips made it survivable.

One of my favourite people at the Park View was an old black guy called John Caldwell Bracy who lived in room 110. He was 80 years old and a World War 2 veteran who had taken to smoking crack cocaine in his dotage. Before it was a hotel, the building had been a low grade rooming house and John was the last surviving remnant of authentic Harlem on the premises, having refused to be a part of the mass exodus some years ago. His tiny room was often chock full of neighbourhood crack whores with names like Daisy, Laverne and Monique, particularly on the first day of the month when he got his army pension. When I once asked him for a reference as to the moral integrity of one of the girls, he replied, "How the hell would I know…? All I know is they sell their pussies and they smoke crack..!"

June came around and Linda hit town with a platonic male friend in tow. Dan was a nice guy whom I had met before in L.A but his presence was logistically undesirable at the very least. I had waited 6 long months to reclaim her heart in a blaze of glory and I didn't need a gooseberry barring my way. As per my recommendation, they checked in at the Park View so at least she was plausibly positioned for my intended seduction.

On the first night, I got rid of the chaperone and took Linda to meet some friends in a hipster bar in the trendy part of Brooklyn near the north end of Bedford Avenue. John and Erin had also been a part of the 3 Ducks story and hailed from Miami but had moved east when Erin landed a place at NYU. We had only been reunited by virtue of a chance meeting on 6th Avenue and West 11th Street a few weeks earlier. They were intrinsically good people although their relationship wouldn't survive the summer as things transpired.

When John and Erin left at around midnight, I gave Linda both barrels of my oft planned romantic offensive. Since leaving L.A, not a day had passed when I hadn't thought of her. And now I had traversed the Atlantic Ocean in the mere hope of caressing her buttermilk velvet skin once more. She seemed flattered and touched or at least flattered enough to be touched as we made out in a dimly lit corner of the bar. We had a lot to talk about, or at least I did, and it was 4.30am when we spilled onto the street shortly before sunrise. True to form, I pushed my luck and suggested we become fully intimate when we got back to the hostel. Linda balked. She was seeing somebody back home and had a typically spurious idea of where the line of infidelity might be drawn. At this point, I threw my toys out in spectacular fashion like a 24 carat brat. As a child she had been abused by an older brother, a painful secret divulged to me with due caution. Unforgivably, I said:

"Fine, stick to having sex with members of your own family. It's what you're good at..!"

Although I quickly apologised and made a fuss of her as she moved to walk away, the damage was done. We retired to our separate rooms and didn't see each other at all the next day. Things were not going according to plan but I wasn't about to give up just yet. On Linda's last night at the Park View, I ushered her to the roof garden and launched into a passionate acoustic rendition of 'Boys Don't Cry.'

'I WOULD SAY I'M SORRY
IF I THOUGHT THAT IT WOULD
CHANGE YOUR MIND

BUT I KNOW THAT THIS TIME
I HAVE SAID TOO MUCH
BEEN TOO UNKIND.'

Linda was a sucker for a song and it seemed to pave the way for a lovely evening, drinking beer and canoodling in the basement while I performed intermittently for the usual suspects. That night we slept in the same bed on the strict condition that I didn't overstep the mark. Confined to the solitude of his own bed, Dan the gooseberry appeared ever so slightly non plussed. He was probably harbouring a sizeable crush of his own and might have thought that this would be the weekend on which he got lucky.

In the morning, not wishing for too poignant a farewell, it was agreed that I would see her off as far as Penn Station on her way to the airport. Dan was booked on a different flight, which was fine by me. As we prepared to say goodbye on the platform at 34 St, she remarked, "So..last night was good..."

"Yeah, it was," I agreed. "Take care of yourself…"

As the train pulled away, I didn't turn around to wave and would never see her again.

22/ SAN FRANCISCO

In the first week of July - despite Caroline's trepidation - Ed came to pay me a visit. After the collapse of my Mills and Boon fairytale, I had never been gladder to see his sculpted crimson coiffure. He was, in fact, a little worried that his avant garde punk style might make him a target in the ghetto but incurring criticism from strangers on account of one's aesthetic is chiefly a British thing, when all said and done. Accustomed to the chav hostility of his native Norbiton, the worst he would encounter in Harlem was a blizzard of compliments from large gregarious black women, proclaiming, "I love that colour...!"

Upon his arrival, we spent a couple of days busking on the F Line before hatching a hair brained scheme to strike it rich at the tables in Atlantic City. In the course of his egotistical ramblings, Manchester Mark had told of the time he allegedly won 12 thousand dollars using a failsafe roulette system before shagging a porn star/ supermodel hybrid and returning to NYC in a helicopter so as not to miss his next shift at the youth hostel. Being a public spirited chap, he explained the basic tenets of the system to me, whilst presumably hoping that material wealth wouldn't change me for the worse.

Armed with this dangerous knowledge, we took the 2 and half hour bus ride to A.C, initially rolling up at the Claridge Casino where our conditions of carriage entitled us to $15 worth of free chips. In the late 80s/ early 90s, Atlantic City had briefly usurped Las Vegas as the Mecca of big time boxing, staging Tyson - Spinks amongst other blockbusters. Beyond that fact, any further comparison was tantamount to a beauty contest between Naomi Campbell and Diane Abbot. Save for the 13 Hotel Casinos situated on the boardwalk, one could find little besides cracked pavements, pool halls and pawn shops.

After losing our free spin at the Claridge, we switched to the Trump Taj Majal as it was easily the most baroque establishment in a town that Reg Gutteridge once described as 'Southend with slot machines.' With its opulent - if rather pretentious - design, at least Donald's gaff offered the illusion of impending riches. Exchanging $200 for gaming chips, we plotted up at a random table, unsure of the standard etiquette but wide eyed and willing to learn. A corset clad cocktail waitress who had perhaps seen better days came past yelling:

"COFFEE, SODA....."

"Can we not get a drop of something more civilised..?" I asked.

"Of course you can, sweetie. I'm just not allowed to advertise the good stuff."

All drinks in American casinos are free for blindingly obvious reasons that the UK never seems to have cottoned onto. I ordered two double whisky and cokes and made a toast to our good fortune. Regrettably, the only aspect of Mark's 'system' that rang true was his assertion that the first column (numbers 1-12) was the 'cold dozen' and the ball would drop more frequently between 13 - 24 or 25 - 36. For some reason, this appeared to be so although I have no idea why. Aside from that, his calculations were about as accurate as William Burroughs' archery skills. Realising that we would likely be broke within half an hour if we continued to follow his advice, I suggested a change of tack.

My plan was simple enough. We bet 15 dollars on every spin. 10 dollars on the dozen that we fancied and 5 dollars on our second choice as a hedge bet. That way, we would double our stake, lose it entirely or break even on every single spin, with only a 33 percent chance of losing. For the benefit of any gambling anoraks, I will concede that the zero and the double zero mildly impacted on those figures but - with such a non committal strategy - it was possible to remain at the table for several hours drinking free booze. Having never previously been intrigued by fiscal games of chance, I was suddenly enthralled with the mathematical drama of it all. At one point, we were up by 200 dollars but it was very much a case of swings and roundabouts with diminishing returns. Taking one strategic break to drink a half bottle of Southern Comfort on the shore, we didn't lose all our money until 11pm or thereabouts.

As we waited outside the Sands Casino for a bus back to New York in the dead of night, Ed had become morose and uncommunicative. Attempting to raise his spirits, I mentioned that I still had 50 cents and suggested we feed it to a one armed bandit in a last gasp attempt to get lucky. He wasn't keen but since we had almost an hour to wait for the next service, I argued that it was better than doing nothing. We walked through the lobby and onto the gaming floor where I shoved a quarter into the first unattended machine. I pulled the lever and nothing happened. Then I put our last 25 cents in and a deluge of silver coins began pouring into the undertray like torrential rain. Gleefully, we embraced and jumped in the air with sufficient gusto to draw curious glances from adjacent gamblers. When I counted the spoils it turned out we had made such a song and dance over the princely sum of $13.50. But at least it would buy breakfast in the morning.

The next day, I tried to be as polite as possible when Mark asked how we had got on with his ingenious 'system.' In our absence, his much talked about girlfriend had checked in and would be in town for a few days before heading to San Francisco. Claire was blonde, big breasted and bore a plausible resemblance to the glamour model, Nell McAndrew. She seemed pleasant enough but I was unaware that I had made an impression on her. Later that night, we attended a Harlem rooftop party at which Ed pulled a delectable mixed race girl who lived in the building and took an instant shine to a cute English punk rock boy with bright red hair. On the drunken subway ride back from 134st, he suddenly announced, "I can't be with Caroline anymore."

Ed's new squeeze joined us the following evening at the 'Knitting Factory' in TriBeCa where an obscure experimental British band called 'Add N To X.' happened to be playing. The support act were midway through their set when Claire entered the venue, accompanied by half a dozen or so of the Park View regulars but with Mark conspicuously not among them. There was no way on earth that she or anyone else had even heard of the band, never mind been a fan of their transiently hip cacophony. Whatever she was after, it had nothing to do with the arty racket that perforated our eardrums for the next 45 minutes.

After the gig, our collective gang sat at a table in the bar area and I noticed that Claire was continually staring and smiling in my direction. I went to the gents and found her waiting in the vestibule when I came out. "I'm drunk enough to say this," she began, "and I'm going to San Francisco on Tuesday, in any case. I think you're really cute." I asked about Mark. "We're not really getting on and that will be over on Tuesday, too." It wasn't as if Mark and I were blood brothers and he had given us terrible financial advice, I reminded myself. We 'snogged' for a while before rejoining the others and exhibiting our newfound intimacy without remorse.

At the end of the night, Ed went back to Meg's apartment and I stayed at John and Erin's place in Crown Heights after bidding Claire goodnight. They had a friend from Miami who lived in the apartment above and desired to rent her spare room, so I moved in that weekend. It was the most racially segregated neighbourhood I had ever seen with an exclusively black contingent on one side of Eastern Parkway and a concentration of Hasidic Jews on the other. John, Erin and Nicole genuinely appeared to be the only white inhabitants on the chiefly Jamaican side.

It was at a Sunday night hostel keg party when Claire admitted that she had to followed me to the gig and invited the others in order to create the illusion of casual coincidence. Although in attendance, Mark seemed oblivious to what was going on between us. "You should come to San Francisco." she said. I explained that my financial situation was somewhat hand to mouth and I would struggle to raise the fare. "I'll lend it to you," she beamed. It turned out she was an exotic dancer who had spent the last few years stripping her way around the world. She and her long term sidekick, Michelle, had given America, Europe, The Antipodes and Far East the benefit of their raw assets in recent times. Now they had rented an apartment in San Francisco and Michelle was already in residence, doing her turn at 'The Roaring 20s' on Broadway. Admittedly, I was warming to the idea of another trip to the West

Coast.

After Ed went home and fell back into the warm confines of his relationship with Caroline, I flew to San Francisco in early August. My flight got in at 11am and I took a taxi to the address that Claire had given me, arriving to find both girls sprawled on couches and complaining of terrible hangovers. Despite the human debris, it was a smart luxury studio that came with a communal gym and outdoor jacuzzi from which the famous Golden Gate Bridge was visible. There was only one double bed in the property, leading me to assume that they probably shared it under normal circumstances.

Small talk ensued as they continued to huddle under blankets, alluding to the shenanigans of night before. Eventually, Claire deigned to get up and made coffee. "I'm getting too old for this drinking," she sighed. So far as I knew, she had reached the ripe old age of 26. For her part, Michelle was a dark haired Irish girl, chatty and amiable but not the kind of overt babe one might associate with her stock in trade. When she left later that afternoon to start her shift at the club, I realised precisely how little Claire and I had to say to each other. In the cold light of day, I wasn't enormously attracted to her, despite the Loaded Magazine stereotype that she approximated. Whether I liked it or not, I was stuck with her for the week and already had cold feet.

I spent the next few days doing the rounds, going to bars and meeting various of Claire and Michelle's friends. The funniest and most agreeable was Sandra from Romford, a short feisty blonde chick who worked as an escort. Sandra liked drinking and playing forfeit games that always seemed to involve the loser getting naked. Being as I was usually outnumbered by females on a basis of 3-1, it wasn't the most lamentable situation. But although I went through the motions, I still wasn't feeling it with Claire.

A visit to Haight - Ashbury confirmed my misgivings. As we walked by the Red Victorian Hotel, I tried to explain how the hallowed street had once been the epicentre of the 60s counter culture but she just wasn't getting it. We had nothing in common and I had come 3000 miles - at her expense - only to discover that she did about as much for my libido as Margaret Thatcher did for the mining industry. It was, of course, all my fault for being such an ego driven, free loading bastard.

On my last night in the city, I went to a bar with Claire and Michelle where they happened to purchase a bunch of light hearted, novelty sex aids from a machine in the female toilets. One of the products was called 'Climax Control Cream.' Claire waved the tube and giggled, "Are you going to be our guinea pig for this, Ben...?" I didn't have the heart to tell her that climax control was hardly my biggest issue where she was concerned. Back at the pad, they knocked up a lethal vodka based punch and a threesome scenario duly ensued.

Being sandwiched between two young strippers might sound like an ethereal dream to the average man but the truth was less spectacular. The scene that unfolded was a glorified drunken grope fest and for me to depict it in a more literary fashion would be most improper. It's a fact of life that most things are not what they are cracked up to be and invariably look better from a distance. When I woke up in the morning and surveyed the carnage, I merely hoped that I had enough cash for a shuttle to the airport. While hastily getting dressed, I found $12 in the right hand pocket of my black jeans and figured it would cover the fare if not the tip.

Choosing not to wake the girls up, I saw myself out.

23/ CATFIGHTS AND COCKTAILS

Not long after I returned from the Bay Area, Erin split up with John and moved to a place in Williamsburg with my flat mate, Nicole, and another chick called Toni. She squared it with the other girls for me to crash on the sofa and nether one seemed to mind too much. During this period we did a lot of drinking as Erin descended into what I would later recognise as chronic alcoholism. At the time she was working as a barmaid in a 24 hour restaurant in the East Village called 'Around The Clock' which meant I could drink for free when she was on duty. At the end of her shift at 2am, it became our routine to head back to the apartment and drink endless 40s of 'Olde English' malt liquor whilst listening to music until 8 or 9 in the morning.

In my heart of hearts, I knew I had a drink problem and was afraid of going the same way as my old man. At the same time, every ounce of my blood and marrow rebelled against the term 'alcoholic' and the sense of shame it evoked. I was like Charles Bukowski or Keith Richards, I would tell myself. Booze was a necessity for my creative process. The only flaw in such logic what that I hadn't written a new song since the last ice age. One might have thought I had gathered plenty of material on the road but none of it seemed to translate into anything of artistic or commercial worth.

New York was already losing its charm for me when a pair of Boeing 767s crashed into the North and South towers of the World Trade Centre within 15 minutes of each other on a Tuesday morning. Nicole was the first to alert the rest of the household to an unprecedented situation, having herself received a call from a friend. We turned on the TV and soon realised that only 2 channels were still in business, showing endless repeats of the surreal footage alongside body count updates and scenes of devastation on the ground. New York City was on Full Terror Alert. Suddenly, George Bush came on the screen explaining that, "We have been targeted because we are the brightest beacon for freedom and democracy in the world but we will do everything in our power to find those folks responsible."

"That's not why you've been targeted, you silly cunt...!" I exclaimed before hurrying downstairs to buy some beer. When I stepped out onto the street, I could see smoke on the horizon, presumably coming from Lower Manhattan. The local store was Arab owned and an angry black guy was giving the proprietors a bit of grief as I stood in line clutching a 6 pack of Corona. I'd never heard of Osama Bin Laden but the media were saying that he was behind the terrifying effrontery. Alarmingly, the old geezer behind the counter even looked like him. Later that afternoon, they would shut up shop for several days, probably amid fears for their own safety.

The four of us were effectively housebound for a week as everything shut down. When I did return to the subway in the hope of making a few bucks, a nearly tangible veil of grief hung over the city. One gentleman asked me if I could dedicate a song to the victims and, for some reason, I came up with The Smiths' 'Sweet and Tender Hooligan.' It probably wasn't the most appropriate of choices.

'HE WAS A SWEET AND TENDER HOOLIGAN
AND HE SWEARS THAT HE'LL NEVER NEVER
DO IT AGAIN
OF COURSE HE WON'T
NOT UNTIL THE NEXT TIME.'

By now I had decided to return to London just as soon as I could get a flight. I was homesick and tired and singing on trains didn't feel right so soon after the most high profile terrorist attack in world history. I waited 2 weeks for international travel to get back up and running before landing at Heathrow on the morning of Monday October 1. As ever, Malcolm was there for me, along with the attic room at Croft Gardens. I got myself a job in a call centre near Richmond Station that chiefly specialised in cajoling confused pensioners into switching their energy supply and generally settled back into London life.

In need of some action, I got mixed up with a dreadful girl from

Sunbury whose only mitigating charm - besides a modicum of sex appeal - was her gorgeous mixed race daughter. Laura was 21, blonde and woefully lacking in class and refinement. Sophia was 4 years old and utterly adorable. Frequently the former would ask me to babysit the latter so she could go out on the lash with her rabble of friends. I never refused as I was besotted with the little cherub who had minimal contact with her biological father. I wanted kids of my own and wondered if my rudderless lifestyle might preclude me from experiencing parenthood.

On a Friday night in February - 3 days shy of my 32nd birthday - I was in Camden Town for what amounted to a joint celebration with Ed, who had turned 22 the day before. Officially, Laura was my date but a girl who happened to be a workmate of Ed's caught my eye in the Good Mixer. Kat was 20 years old - charismatic, confrontational and constantly spannered on account of her relentless consumption of mid strength lager. When she asked if Laura was my girlfriend, I replied, "Not really…" When she subsequently asked, "In that case can I have a snog…?" I saw no reason not to oblige her.

We moved from the Mixer to the World's End where the bouncers refused to let Kat in unless she ate something first. One of our contingent dashed to a nearby shop and returned with a Cornish pasty which was duly force fed to her in deference to their rather pointless stipulation. Once inside, I all but ditched Laura and hit the dance floor with Kat who hadn't noticeably sobered up despite the compulsory intake of calories. After an extended period of cavorting, I went to the bar for more drinks and somehow got in a fight with 4 or 5 random lads, one of whom had looked at me in a way that I took exception to. I got rather the worst of things but was still spitting defiance and throwing punches when security moved in to break it up.

Quite badly bruised and swollen, I decided to repair with Kat and Laura to a nearby drug den after closing time in order to smoke some heroin. Since kicking the habit back in '99, I would still use gear on an occasional basis, often in league with Ed after a night on the tiles. Our connection was a black guy called Rupert, who lived in Euston and made a living selling used travel cards back in the era when Kings Cross was awash with dealers, prostitutes and conmen. Due to the advent of the oyster card and expanding gentrification, the area bears no resemblance to its former self today.

The following week, I went for drinks with Kat after work in Richmond and invited her back to Croft Gardens where we spent the night together. From that day forward, Laura faded into the background, although I would still look after Sophia whenever requested for the next few months.

As soon as I had taken up with Kat, Ed finally finished with Caroline. As a result, we spent a lot of time hanging out as a trio which quickly led to complications. Kat had a very relaxed attitude towards nudity and sexual intimacy and, under such circumstances, it seemed inevitable that the lines of our relationship would be ill defined. Before I knew it, my best friend and I were both having sex with her which engendered a simmering resentment on my part, if not his. I tried to convince myself that it was harmless bohemian larks but, in truth, I didn't like it. The dynamic would end in tears and effectively denied Kat and myself the opportunity of ever having a normal liaison. Thereafter, I never felt as if I owed her any loyalty.

February 12, 2002 was a fateful day. Opting to skip work on a nameless Tuesday, Kat and I convened at the White Cross by the river. Although I hadn't even sparred for over 10 years, the boxer reputation had stayed with me and I never needed too much of an excuse to bend someone's ears on the subject of 'past glories.' Midway through the second pint, she suddenly said, "Take me to a Boxing show tonight...!" I explained that it wasn't like the opera and that I had no idea if there might be a small hall professional boxing show in the capital that evening. Although I still watched the big fights, I hadn't followed the grass roots scene or bought Boxing News in a couple of years.

Boxing News was our best bet I told her and we could probably pick up a copy from WH Smith's on Richmond High Street. "If you really want to do this then we'd better get out of here now, though," I warned. A few times a year, the area would fall prey to high tide causing water levels to rise above the steps leaving customers stranded inside the pub. More than once, Ed and I had used this natural phenomenon as an excuse not to go back to work after a lunchtime tipple but, as the Thames threatened to become a moat, we necked our drinks and headed for the door.

Walking into Smiths, I picked up a copy of BN in its new broadsheet form and saw that Danny Williams was defending his British and Commonwealth Heavyweight Titles that very night at the legendary York Hall in Bethnal Green. The show was advertised under the promotional banner of 'Eugene Maloney In Association With Don King' and would be televised live on BBC1. It had been quite a few years since the terrestrial giant had deigned to cover boxing and the trade paper headline made due fanfare of that fact. Using Kat's mobile, since I had yet to own one, I called the ticket enquires number. A man who may or may not have been Eugene Maloney - but certainly wasn't Don King - answered. I asked if tickets were available on the door and he replied, "Yes, sir. As long as you get there early. There's 11 fights on and the show starts at 6 O'clock."

The York Hall remains the spiritual home of British Boxing and there is a majesty about its draconian old school facade - with its trio of Edwardian Arches and incongruent red logo. Although I was well aware of the cultural significance, it would be the first time I had actually set foot in the building. We arrived at 6.30pm and purchased 2 standard tickets from the box office before taking our seats just in time to see Enzo Maccarinelli make short work of one James Gilbert via 2nd round TKO. In later years, Enzo would rise to prominence as a British, European and 'world' champion but was perfectly unknown to me at the time.

Amongst the sizeable Welsh contingent in the house was reigning WBO super middleweight champion, Joe Calzaghe, the jewel in the crown of his father's home-grown stable which featured heavily on the card that night. Another future triple champ, Gavin Rees, won a 6 round decision over some oft beaten Ukrainian import whilst Bradley Pryce prevailed in the 9th round of a pulsating war with Gavin Down. To this day, it remains one of the best fights I've ever seen, up close. At one point, I left my seat to grab a word with Calzaghe but found him shy and aloof - seemingly ill at ease with the kind of recognition his confederates were risking their lives to attain.

Flitting to and from the bar at various stages of the evening, I saw a surfeit of old faces. Charlie Magri, Lloyd Honeyghan and Colin McMillan. Joe Ryan who used to train Kirk and Tony Laing at The Becket and even dear old Lester Jacobs who didn't remember me or our sparring session 11 years earlier. Kat was enjoying the ambience but that was almost an irrelevance from my perspective. I felt an immediate sense of belonging that I never got when attending some poxy gig in an overrated North London toilet. This was my world. Why had I turned my back on it and for what...? 2 gigs, 2 recordings, 2 heroin habits and a CRB that resembled a weekly shopping list. I realised that I had no further interest in being in a band and wondered if I wasn't too old to have another go in the ring.

In the main event, Danny Williams had too much for Michael Sprott, who had allegedly been sunning himself on a Caribbean Island when the call came for a late notice payday. It was all over in the 7th round but Michael would have better nights in an up and down career that would see him rack up more air miles than Richard Branson. Regaling in thunderous applause with the magnificent Lonsdale Belt sheathed around his waist, Danny cannot have imagined that punching for pay would eventually cast him as a sacrificial lamb to the kind of 'also rans' he would once have blown away by accident.

24/ WALKING IN THE SAND

Despite the random circumstances of my reintroduction to the world of boxing, my passion had been fully reignited. As a result, Kat and I got to as many shows as we could in the next several months. Danny Williams vs Keith Long back at the York Hall, Audley Harrison vs Dominic Negus at Wembley Conference Centre and Naseem Hamed's desultory swan song at the London Arena. Despite the 'Fresh Prince' tag, Naz seemed to have lost the magic and the most rousing cheer of the night went to Page 3 girl, Leilani Dowding, as she hoisted a placard, mercifully signifying the start of the last round. By that point, as much as 30 percent of the crowd had already left the building.

By degrees, I moved out of Croft Gardens and into the 4 bed roomed house that Kat shared with her mother in Clerkenwell. The latter was a fine, intelligent and fair minded lady but perhaps a little permissive of her daughter's more wanton excesses. Since the untimely death of her father when she was 13, Kat appeared to have concocted a persona both brazen and promiscuous in an effort to block out her undigested grief. The first time I was invited to the house she had strode into the lounge topless, on some unimportant premise, causing her mother to plead, "COVER YOURSELF UP, FOR GOODNESS SAKE..!" Ultimately, the liberal tolerance probably worked in my favour. Had Kat's Mum been of a more severe persuasion, it's unlikely she would have allowed a 32 year old drifter to take up residence in the first place.

During this period, Kat and I both worked for a company in Hoxton called IFF Research, conducting various government surveys about all manner of spurious nonsense. Shifts were booked on a weekly basis, which suited us down to the ground and if we felt like a day on the piss then we took it without penance or parental censure. In many ways, it was an idyllic time of life although the fudged axis between Kat, Ed and myself remained a bone of contention. The situation finally exploded during a trip to Paris in the summer when I put Ed in casualty and obliterated a hotel room door in the midst of a mutual gin bender. That the manager of said establishment resembled a Moroccan version of Mike

Tyson was simply my misfortune as we tried to make a discreet exit in the morning.

Back home, I would return the favour in predictable fashion, when I briefly inveigled Kat's best friend into our sex life during the endless lost weekends on Sekforde Street. Something tells me she would not appreciate a name check in these pages but, for the reader's benefit, she was Turkish, dark haired and agreeably pretty. But although I continued to tick off a clichéd bucket list of decadent landmarks, I still had no real idea of what I wanted to do with my life. What I did know was that I was growing weary of London, once more.

Islington and its neighbouring borough of Hackney were infested with hordes of little chav millennials who would frequently hurl abuse at any person who deviated from their Reebok Classics aesthetic. Kat's outlandish dress sense that espoused luminous leg warmers, micro skirts and boxing boots seemed to serve as a beacon for this kind of impromptu criticism and I was beginning to tire of the aggravation encountered on our walks to and from work. I had a lot of unfulfilled aggression and concluded that geography was to blame. Following a familiar pattern, I suggested we take a trip to New York.

Although her mum wasn't keen, Kat liked the idea and so we began to save our weekly wages whilst putting in a few extra shifts at IFF. Within 8 weeks, we had flights to JFK booked for Tuesday, November 19. It was a month before our departure when I was reading the Metro in my call booth and noted that Audley Harrison was due to contest his 8th professional bout on the undercard of the Gatti - Ward rematch in Atlantic City on November 23. Back in May, Arturo Gatti and Micky Ward had staged what some observers still regard as the greatest fight in boxing history. And here was the encore taking place on the East Coast within 4 days of our arrival. Calling out to Kat who was seated opposite, I said, "Guess where we're going….?" I tossed the paper onto her desk and she knew it made sense. That night we called the box office at the Boardwalk Hall and bought two $50 tickets for our first American boxing show.

Our flight landed late on the Tuesday night so we took a subway train to midtown, then a cab to Jazz on the Park on W 106th Street. As per normal in waking hours, Kat was drunk and stared out of the back windscreen as we passed through Times Square like a 6 year old seeing Blackpool Illuminations for the first time. The Park View would have been my first choice of a place to stay but it had ceased to be a hostel since my last visit and turned back into some kind of social housing project. Jazz on the Park was equitable in price but soul destroyingly commercial and overrun by groups of Latino school children.

With 3 days to go until the fight, I caught up with old acquaintances and introduced Kat to New York as I knew it. Luc was in his sophomore year at Eugene Lang and had moved from Jersey City to Brooklyn. Erin still lived in the apartment on Bushwick Avenue but had gotten sober at some point since we were last aquatinted. She had the AA symbol of unity tattooed on her left forearm and had lost a fair bit of weight due to a rigid low carb diet that involved weighing her food, even when dining out. She seemed a lot happier but it would be many years before I understood why. Despite the change of identity, Robert and Big Steve still ran the Park View and Old John was still in room 110, hitting a stone at every opportunity and trying to get his 80 year old appendage sucked.

At 10am on the Saturday morning, we boarded a coach to Atlantic City from outside the Upper West Side deli that sold us the tickets. As I'd noted on the previous trip with Ed, most of our fellow passengers were over 60 and approximated the white trash stereotype. Unlike Vegas, A.C was not regarded as a cool place for youngsters to frequent, either for impulsive matrimonial ceremonies or bacchanalian stag dos. Arriving at lunchtime, we headed straight for the Taj Mahal and won $40 on our first venture at the tables. "See how easy it is..?" I said. "And the drinks are free, too."

Inevitably, beginners luck didn't last and we started to take a kicking, mitigated only by the continuous supply of 'free' whisky and cokes. After several losses on the spin, we decided to turn it in and explore the surrounding terrain. We invested in a disposable camera and took pictures on the boardwalk before visiting a few of the local dive bars. In one Irish watering hole somebody said that Gatti had failed to make the weight and had to remove his underwear to come in under 140. He didn't understand how Arturo's boxer shorts could have weighed as much as the initial discrepancy, he added.

At 7pm, we took our place in the queue outside the Boardwalk Hall, only to be told that we couldn't take a camera into the venue. It was irritating but, not wanting to lose our photos, we walked to the beach and buried the Kodak Flash in the sand, carefully counting our steps in order to pinpoint its precise location for retrieval. Admitted at the second time of asking, we were escorted to our seats way up in the Gods as an up and coming welterweight by the name of Anthony 'The Messenger' Thompson was introduced to a threadbare crowd. I wasn't expecting inner ringside for 50 bucks but, from where we were situated, the scene resembled an aerial colour photograph of Dempsey - Carpentier.

With the arena being mostly empty, I suggested we move down into the section near the ring for a better view of the undercard. Thompson halted his outgunned opponent in the second round, making way for another undefeated welterweight called Freddie Cedena who somewhat laboured to an 8th round stoppage over one Bradley Jensen. Two fights later, Jensen would be KOd by Thompson inside 3 rounds. As people began to arrive in greater numbers, whenever somebody said we were in their seats, we simply shuffled a few places to the left or right. One fighter who caught my eye was Paulie Malignaggi, a brash light welterweight prospect from Brooklyn with leopard print trunks and blonde streaks. Exhibiting shades of an orthodox Hector Camacho, he was adjudged a split decision winner over the useful Paul Delgado who had evidently impressed one of the ringside arbiters more than he had me.

By the time Audley Harrison dispatched a Glenn Catley look-alike called Shawn Robinson after 2 minutes and nine seconds of the opening round, the hall was full to capacity and Michael Buffer had assumed his duties on the mic. "Sort it out, Audley..!" shrieked Kat, cutting a fine figure in her red PVC mini skirt bearing the image of Sid Vicious on the crotch. Despite being obliged to move about 30 times, we were still sitting pretty in the $250 section when the principals entered the ring.

In relative contrast to the first fight, Gatti boxed beautifully, making better use of his superior skills at range. In the 3rd round, a counter right hand sent Ward careering face first into the turnbuckle of his opponent's corner. Arising on unsteady legs, he absorbed the subsequent barrage like the warrior he had always been and even finished the round on top as the evenly divided crowd hollered its rambunctious approval. At the conclusion of a sequel only marginally less breathtaking than its predecessor, Gatti's revenge was confirmed by majority decision. "They're both hard as NAILS," marvelled Kat as we headed for the exit.

Outside, a large portion of the crowd walked into the adjacent Caesar's Palace while Kat and I went to look for our camera in the sand. Painstakingly retracing our steps in accordance with the alignment of the stars we arrived at the designated spot and found a half bottle of Seagram's Gin where the camera ought to have been. It seemed inconceivable that anyone would steal a 10 dollar camera and leave 35 centilitres of liquor in compensation. And if we had gotten our directions wrong then it was awfully coincidental that we had stumbled on someone else's contraband. Whatever the explanation, there was no sense in wasting a decent drop of gin.

25/ GLEASON'S

On the Monday after the fight, Kat and I paid a visit to the legendary Gleason's Gym on Front St, in an area of Brooklyn known as the D.U.M.B.O. As we entered, a young guy of Latin appearance with peroxide blonde highlights in his shock of dark spiky hair was seated on the steps adjoining one of 4 rings. It turned out to be my new favourite 140 pounder, Paulie Malignaggi. Dressed in a casual tracksuit, he seemed pleasantly surprised at being recognised by a bohemian looking English couple whose names he took to be 'Benny and Katz.' When I cited the Camacho comparison, he replied, "Everybody says that. I got one of his old trainers, Billy Giles." Referring to his fight at the weekend, he said that Delgado had been "a dirty fighter. He was buttin' me all night. "

Also in the gym were former 2 weight 'world' champion turned trainer, Joey Gamache, and recently crowned WBA regular champ, 'Vicious' Vivian Harris. Harris was trained by Lennox Blackmore who had fought Aaron Pryor and Antonio Cervantes back in the day. Mingling freely with the large contingent of mostly black and Hispanic pros was a surfeit of 'white collar' enthusiasts, male and female. Gleason's owner, Bruce Silverglade was credited with pioneering the white collar boxing boom, although the rise of the sport's popularity amongst the more genteel stratum of society can actually be traced back to James Figg in the early 18th century.

Having not trained in 12 years, save for shadow boxing in the shower, I purchased some boxing boots and joined up for a month. The rigours of skipping, bag work and groundwork provided a welcome antidote to the years of chemical abuse and I loved being around the fighters and peripheral characters who hung around the gym. In the first week, I bumped into former champion, Junior Jones who told me he was fighting in a few days time 'on pay per view.' He was actually appearing on the Christy Martin - Mia St. John undercard and dropped a wide 10 round decision to an obscure Colombian named Ivan Alvarez. The following Monday, his veteran trainer, Bob Jackson told me that Junior was 'all shot.' Evidently, Jones agreed with him and never fought again.

At this point, I wanted a life in boxing but wasn't sure how it could be facilitated. With such convenient access, it occurred to me that I could possibly conduct a few interviews with fighters and trainers but I had no idea that any platform for such things existed on the internet. My best guess was that I could send the copy to Claude Abrams at Boxing News and maybe he would print it. A few months ago we had met in the toilets at York Hall and he seemed open to freelance contributions. On this journalistic premise, I asked Bruce Silverglade if he knew the notorious Mitch 'Blood' Green.

"Sure," he answered.

"Is he an approachable guy..?"

"On the street, I'm sure he's a bum but he always behaves himself in here. Give him a call. He's a ham... He likes the attention."

He scrawled the fighter's number on a scrap of paper and handed it to me. Thanking him, I resolved to give 'Blood' call in the next few days to break the ice.

To save on hostel bills, we went to stay with Meg for a week in her apartment on 137th and Broadway, in a section of Harlem that was heavily populated by Dominicans and Puerto Ricans. Confusingly, it wasn't Spanish Harlem on the East Side which seemed to be more black dominated in that era. Meg had been Ed's holiday romance back in 2001 and since her roommates were away in Mississippi, she invited to us 'come and hang' for a few days.

On the first night of this temporary arrangement, she and I ended up getting into it whilst Kat was passed out on the sofa after a typically hepatotoxic evening of indulgence. Suddenly, before things went too far, she scurried to her room topless, insisting, "This is SO wrong. Your girlfriend's asleep right there...!" I wanted to explain that Kat and I had a more flexible kind of relationship but the window of opportunity had clearly come and gone. Throughout December, I kept up my workouts at Gleason's although I wasn't seriously thinking about fighting again at the time. I was still drinking alcoholically but made an effort to cut down on the fags to improve my cardio. Although she was looking for a job, Kat didn't seem greatly interested in anything besides getting slaughtered every night. In all fairness to her, that's what we had always done.

As Christmas approached, I gently suggested that Kat might like to go home to recharge her batteries while I held the fort. Briefly, we had joined the workforce at Jazz On The Park but soon found the regular cleaning and laundry duties unbearable, even in exchange for free board. There was no question that I was an active alcoholic at the time but there was something about the way Kat drank which seemed to trump everything. It was almost possible to hide my drink problem behind her more screaming issues that took centre stage. She had no qualms about drinking first thing in the morning and was the kind of drunk who liked to tell people about themselves. Her sharp tongue combined with a strong intellectual firmament meant that she was frequently hilarious but only up to a point. And on a daily basis, it got old.

My motion was carried and Kat flew home from JFK shortly before Christmas. I saw her off at the gate but later learned that she had been adjudged too inebriated to board her designated flight and was ordered to sober up and wait for the next one. After her departure, I checked in at a hostel in Spanish Harlem called the 'Manhattan Youth Castle' which cost $90 for 6 nights. Every guest was given a key and the management would leave at 6pm every day, essentially trusting us to look after the place. Officially, alcohol was not allowed on the premises but everyone knew the score and would simply tidy away the evidence of night-time revelry.

The New York winter was excruciatingly cold, above and beyond anything the UK was capable of serving up. By the week of Yuletide, there was 3 feet of the snow on the ground, making it necessary to proceed down the slope of Lexington Avenue with due caution. As romantic as it might have been, I felt quite sad and lonely. I missed Kat more than I had expected and was fed up with singing on trains day after day. 2 days before Christmas Eve, I briefly found comfort in the company of a young Canadian girl whom I had taken along with her friend to a red neck bar on the Upper West Side known as 'Yogi's. But transient fumbles in the common room did nothing to dispel the sense of emptiness.

Whatever I might have been looking for, it remained invisible.

26/ BLOOD

On a cold night in January, I finally came face to face with Mitch Green after a slew of inconclusive conversations over the phone. I'd had a fascination with Green and his reputation as a former gang leader since reading about him as a teenager in American fight magazines. I was particularly intrigued about reports that a gas station in the Bronx had once gone through more than 100 staff members in 6 months, such was the daily terrorism that the fighter had subjected them to. In 1986 he became the second man to go the distance with a ferocious young Mike Tyson but was more world famous for the notorious early morning street spat outside Dapper Dan's in Harlem.

Mitch liked the idea that a 'journalist' from England wanted to talk to him but would constantly ask, "Am I gonna' make any money outta' this...?" I told him that it wasn't about money and I didn't have any but eventually agreed to pay him $50, despite having no deal in place for the interview. I took the subway to Archer Avenue in Queens before boarding something called the Rosedale Dollar Van which took people out to areas in the projects not served by regular public transport. Sardined in the back of the vehicle, I noted that I was the only white person with occasion to be travelling to South Jamaica that evening.

Mitch had simply told me that he lived at 110/24 which didn't make complete sense to me but when we approached 110th Avenue, I asked for the driver to stop and let me out. The dark streets were deserted as I tried to establish a sense of direction in accordance with the house numbers on what appeared to be a very long road. I kept the hood of my green Parka coat up, partly because it was cold but also to hide my ethnicity. On reflection, it was probably a pointless ruse, since not too many young Afro American gang bangers wore leather trousers, to the best of my knowledge. Eventually, I came to a row house located between 110/22 and 110/26 and figured it was the one I was looking for, despite having no visible number affixed. A rusted old Cadillac in the driveway lent more credence to that assumption.

I pressed the doorbell and discovered that it wasn't working. On the opposite side of the street, I saw a light on in the front room of a house that appeared to be occupied by a decent God fearing black family so I rang the bell and asked if they knew which house was number 110/24. A lady in her 50s wearing a red towelled bathrobe answered.

"What's the name...?"

"Mitch Green," I told her.

"What's your name...?"

"Ben..."

She picked up her landline phone in the hallway and made a call.

"Yo Blood... Ben's outside. Answer the door..."

I walked back across the street and there he stood in the doorway at the top of the steps. He was everything I imagined to be. A giant of a man in a white sweat suit with trademark jheri curls and a barely decipherable ghetto drawl. He invited me in and motioned for me to sit on the couch while he reclined in an armchair near the archway that led to the kitchen. Above said archway was a piece of laminated card bearing the inscription 'MITCH "BLOOD" GREEN - FIGHTING MACHINE.'

I gave him the 50 bucks up front and turned on the dictaphone I had borrowed from a South African kid at the Youth Castle. He explained how he had risen to prominence on the streets of the Bronx as the leader of a gang called the 'Black Warriors.' The dreadlocked black guy who gets shot at the beginning of the iconic 'Warriors' movie was based on him he insisted. He had been directed to boxing by a mentor in a detention centre and won 4 New York Golden Gloves before turning pro with Shelley Finkel. Mike Tyson was a closet queer who had had won their fight at The Garden purely because everything was stacked in his favour, not least the purse split. Don King was a 'no good faggot' who had robbed him silly and recanted on a catalogue of promises. He gave me his account of the infamous street brawl, alleging that Tyson had instigated the physical confrontation, only to flee the scene with his bodyguards.

The previous year, Mitch had beaten a journeyman called Danny Wofford in a Virginia High School for something called the World Boxing Syndicate Super Heavyweight Inaugural 'World' Title. "That's a load of bollocks..!" I told him, "How can you consider yourself a world champion after beating a guy with 92 fucking losses...?"

"Hey, it's a belt, man..." he shot back. "The other champs won't fight me."

"Mitch, you were a good fighter but you are 46 years old..."

"I'm in great shape...!" he bellowed before jumping out of the chair and shadow boxing frenetically as if to prove that he was ready to take on Lennox Lewis there and then. After about 90 minutes, I turned the tape off and got up to leave. "I'm glad I met you, man," said Mitch 'Blood' Green.

"You too, champ, be lucky."

As I walked down the street he yelled, "Wait, you didn't get to see the belt..." He disappeared from view momentarily and returned wearing the bland grey bauble he had annexed by virtue of beating 'Experienced' Danny Wofford, posturing with pride. I told him he would always be a champion to me and walked all the way back to Archer Avenue buzzing with excitement.

In mid January, I met a girl from Albuquerque who represented herself as a budding screen writer and author. In her daytime winter garb, Cammy would not have turned heads but the night-time saw her take on a more vampish appearance as she scrubbed up and took to the streets after midnight. To those in the communal dorms who couldn't help noticing her irregular routine, she claimed to be doing night research for a law firm in the City. Soon after we bonded, she told me the truth regarding her nocturnal work commitments:

"I hope you don't think bad of me but if I've been working as an escort..." she started.

"I've done a lot of things in my life and I'm not in the business of judgement," I told her.

"Ben, I like you. When I get an apartment, you can come and stay with me," she promised.

For the next few weeks, we became thick as thieves although there was nothing sexual going on. Being obliged to split proceeds down the middle with her Puerto Rican lady pimp, Cammy was earning $150 per client and would often turn up to 3 tricks a night. Frequently, she should take me to breakfast or lunch in order to offload some of the stories regarding the more bizarre carnal hankerings of her customers. One guy was sufficiently old that he could no longer have sex but liked to slap women around. On top of the basic rate, she got a tip every time the octogenarian weirdo cuffed her. He was known as 'The Hitter' and she didn't relish his appointments.

Impulsively one Saturday afternoon, I went back to Mitch Green's house with Cammy and her camcorder as she captured the upshot on film. The resulting conversation can be seen on YouTube today and continues to draw comments, 17 years after the fact. A week later, she hired a limo for my 33rd birthday and we cruised around Manhattan to the contrasting strains of NWA and The Smiths with selected members of our international peer group. Our dynamic suddenly turned sour when we crossed the line of innocent friendship the night before we were due to move into a high rise apartment in the Columbia district. Having expected to get the keys on the day in question, Cammy booked us a room at the Malibu Hotel opposite the new apartment building and one thing lead to another after we shared a bottle of Jack Daniels. The next morning, her whole attitude towards me seemed to change. I could stay for a while at the new pad, she said, but shouldn't get too comfortable as the place wasn't big enough for the both of us.

In the light of her concerns about spatial restrictions, it seemed odd that she invited an annoying Aussie chick from the hostel to share the floor space with us. Clearly, it was a strategic move to insert a wedge between us and the intimacy that had been building. The remainder of February was no fun whatsoever with the ambience being very much 'girls against boy.' When Cammy then forged a romance with a young Italian kid called Lorenzo, I felt as if I was living behind enemy lines. I was pissed off and suddenly had an overwhelming desire to fight again.

27/ VICIOUS

I renewed my membership at Gleason's on Monday, March 3, 2003. 2 days earlier, Roy Jones had beaten John Ruiz to capture the WBA heavyweight title and the gym was awash with talk that maybe Roy could beat a faded Mike Tyson, too. In November, I had trained with enthusiasm but this time it was different. I became a man possessed, seemingly on a mission to claw back the wasted years of dissolute indulgence in their entirety. I worked out 6 days a week and only took a break on Sunday's because the gym wasn't open on the Sabbath. I stopped drinking, save for a couple of pints of Guinness now and then, and cut out smoking altogether.

One afternoon, I had just finished a few rounds on the heavy bag and Joey Gamache remarked, "You look good out there. Nice combinations…"

Flattered, I said, "It means something, coming from you, Joey."

"I can tell you know how to fight," he replied.

Buoyed by the endorsement of a former world champ, I asked how much it would cost for me to do a bit or work with him. "I charge 25 dollars a session. I don't do it by the hour," he explained. I began training with Joey on a pay as you go basis and found him to be a good coach and a prince among men. He gave me the combination to his locker in case I needed to use any equipment when he wasn't there and related many an interesting story of his illustrious career. He had been Mike Tyson's roommate at the Olympic Trials and admitted that Julio Cesar Chavez had provided his biggest payday. "Julio really knew how to walk you down," he conceded.

When Joey saw how serious I was about boxing again, he became reluctant to take my money: "I hate to charge a guy who's gonna' fight. How about I just give you some mitt work when I have time and you have my locker number if you need anything." It was Joey who set up my first sparring session since I had stormed out of the Becket a dozen years ago with a Guyanese light heavyweight called John Douglas. John had represented his country at the Atlanta Olympics and was nobody's fool but had been used in the

paid ranks, resulting in 8 losses from 13 fights. My movement and timing seemed pretty good after such a hiatus but, 3 rounds in, I hit the wall and wanted to regurgitate. I spat out my mouthpiece, involuntarily, prompting John Douglas to shout, "ONE MORE... WITH COURAGE...!" I got through another hellish 3 minutes and Joey said, "Thanks, John. You really know how to work a guy."
"I'm not a fucking idiot," replied the fighter, lest it was in doubt.

A couple of days later, I sparred with a tough Irish light middleweight by the name of Connor Higgins with a 5 and 4 record. He reacquainted me with the crippling discomfort of a decent body shot but I didn't do too badly and it gave me a lift when former WBO champion, Agapito Sanchez, told me "You have nice combinations. " Connor had a 4 rounder coming up in Atlantic City and asked me to spar for 3 days of the following week. I improved each time and came close to working him over in the last session. Perhaps I was galvanised by the fact that the legendary Emile Griffith had gloved me up on that occasion.

I was still busking to earn my corn and would typically work Line F on my way to the gym, getting off at York Street. Bruce allowed me to pay my gym fees in instalments and would keep my guitar in the office while I trained. On the home front, Cammy and I resolved our differences but when a room became available at Meg's place in West Harlem, I hit the street running. My other housemate was an attractive Vietnamese girl called Diana and Meg rented the fourth bedroom to a pair of drug dealers from the block who answered to Cornell and Pablo respectively. They didn't live in the apartment but used the room as their little bunker in which to hold court.

One day, I arrived at the gym and a Guyanese trainer called Colin asked me, "Would you throw a few punches at my fighter...?" His fighter turned out to be a strapping black cruiserweight who I had seen before but wasn't sure of the name. We did 3 rounds during which he was nice and respectful, working on speed and technique without taking liberties. As I was getting out of the ring, Colin informed me, "You just sparred with the world champion."

He turned out to be Wayne Braithwaite, who had won the vacant WBC cruiserweight strap the previous October. I felt 10 feet tall and treated myself to a single Guinness in Yogi's on the way home. When I later told a friend that I had shared the ring with a world champ and pointed to his name in The Ring ratings for authenticity, he asked, "How can he be the world champion when he's only rated No.3…?" That was a long story for another day, I explained.

By late April, Paul Malignaggi was back in the gym, having recovered from a recurring hand injury. I pestered Billy Giles for a few rounds with his charge and he acquiesced one day, allowing me to mix in with 3 other guys, 2 rounds apiece. I already knew that he was quick and slick and wasn't showing me his A game but I acquitted myself sufficiently well for Billy to invite me back for more in subsequent weeks as they readied for a guy called Shad Howard on ESPN. Since the advent of my social media celebrity, a dedicated band of trolls have attempted to depict the Malignaggi sparring sessions as nothing more than a figment of my imagination and cite Paulie's abject lack of recollection as proof. While I am glad that such people have found a niche in life, let me state here and now that we sparred at least 4 times between May and August 2003 and I will happily go blind if I'm lying.

I was in bed one morning when my old mate, Axel, from the Park View phoned to ask if I fancied a bit of removals work and could I get to Greenwich Village in an hour's time…? "You'll make good money, man," he promised. I had known Axel from the previous stay in NY and was aware that he was the foreman of a moving firm called 'Ideal.' I agreed to meet him at the given address and figured I could train in the evening. When I arrived at the apartment block in Barrow Street, I was somewhat surprised to see Axel and a Chicano workforce loading furniture into a vehicle that looked as if it had been mocked up for Liberace's stag week. Bright pink and emblazoned with rainbows it bore a lipstick kiss emblem next to the slogan 'COME ON DARLING, YOU KNOW WE ARE THE BEST..!'

Knowing Axel to be a typical Latin macho type, I thought it best not to say anything and simply mucked in with the others. The customers were clearly a gay couple, moving from one Manhattan address to another, and didn't seem to have a lot of heavy or unwieldy possessions. It was probably the easiest move I had ever done and the tip at the end of the day was way in excess of my expectations. Axel also paid me a day's wages at 10 bucks an hour and told me to meet him at the company depot in the morning.

After a few days of working for exclusively gay and lesbian customers, I realised that Ideal must be a niche company pandering to the pink dollar. I couldn't readily see how the moving needs of a gay person would radically differ from those of their heterosexual counterparts but I wasn't complaining, making $100 dollars a day on average plus a weekly wage on top. Life was getting easier and a plan was coming together.

Because I was white and still looked like a guy who had lost his way to a gig at CBGBs, I started to attract attention from fighters and coaches in the gym and seemed to be in demand for sparring. One time, Lennox Blackmore approached me on the bag and asked, "Will you spar with the champ..?"

"Who, Wayne....?" I wondered.

"Not Wayne," he said sullenly. "Vivian."

"Today...?"

"Not today. Tomorrow."

"Ok, what time...?"

"12 O' Clock...."

Joey Gamache advised me against it. Vivian had a reputation for trying to knock guys out in the gym and he reminded me that, "Once you're in there, you're stuck there..." There was no way I was going to back out as I was too excited about being asked in the first place. In hindsight, I realise that Blackmore chiefly picked me because they wouldn't have to give me any money but, at the time, I saw it as a badge of honour.

The next day, WBA regular champ Vivian Harris did 3 rounds with a white American amateur and 3 with yours truly. With his cachet as a reigning world champ of sorts, the whole gym stopped to watch, encircling the ring expectantly. I was very mindful not to get his rag out by loading up and stayed behind my jab in the first round. In the second round, he nailed me flush in the face with a straight right hand and I acknowledged him with a nod. "You're doing well but you're not throwing enough punches," opined John Douglas. In the last round Harris danced and clowned around for the benefit of some of the hood groupies that formed part of his entourage. When it was over, I walked up to Joey Gamache and said, "Well, that wasn't so terrible...."

"No, you did well," he agreed with just a trace of reluctance.

28/ REDEMPTION

By June, my weight was down to a hundred and fifty four pounds, having been over one - seventy when I first got the hump with Cammy. I was holding my own with good fighters in the gym and doing my roadwork around Harlem and Central Park. I had money in my pocket thanks to the more restless members of New York's Gay and Lesbian community and a new trainer called Moe Sims. Moe was a former nightclub owner who had worked with Junior Jones and a young Riddick Bowe as well as former WBA middleweight champion, Julio Cesar Green. He was a lovely guy but his boxing knowledge didn't strike me as indispensable.

Moe encouraged me to think about turning pro but the Mancunian girl who ran the amateur programme at Gleason's told me that I couldn't get a license with the NYSAC unless I had at least one amateur fight in the U.S. For $16 she could get me a USA Boxing card and would look to match me on her next club show set for July 12, she hastened to add. When she asked about my experience, I told her the truth - 34 fights, 25 wins - more out of ego than honesty. It meant that I would be coming back at open class level which was a tad ridiculous given that my last bona fide contest had taken place in the summer of 1988. I paid the 16 bucks and my license arrived via Colorado Springs about a week later. Soon it was confirmed that I would be fighting Ashantie Hendrickson of Memorial Vets in Long Island on Saturday, July 12 over four - two minute rounds. Hendrickson was 18 and Christine said he never weighed more than a hundred and fifty pounds.

With my life finally starting to gain a semblance of stability, perhaps it was inevitable that I would seek to introduce a familiar element of chaos. I had been talking to Kat back in London and we both decided it would be a marvellous idea if she came back to join me once more. It's hard to imagine what possessed me to think she would be the perfect companion for my final weeks of serious preparation but there we have it. The upshot was that she arrived within days and immediately demonstrated that her priorities had not changed one iota.

Kat landed a job canvassing for some beauty related brand and made a few friends of her own while I readied for war and tried to ignore her habitual drinking and adhesion to marijuana. Things got worse still when Meg's younger brother, Shelby, moved into the apartment. He was a nice enough kid at heart but being 20 years old and coming from Newport, Vermont, he seemed to adopt a persona that was loosely based on Suge Knight as soon as he set foot in the projects. Admittedly, I had no idea how we behaved in his natural habitat but the lad's demeanour seemed contrived at best.

With the introduction of Kat and Shelby, the household chemistry no longer worked and Meg asked us to leave. Consequently, we moved to a 2 bed apartment in the Sunset Park district of Brooklyn, sharing with a black chick of my acquaintance called Niquae. I met Niquae at the Manhattan Youth Castle and she had seemed normal enough at a regular social distance. Restricted to the same confines of bricks and mortar, I soon realised that she was palpably nuts. She had a penchant for walking around the house naked and was inappropriately suggestive to Kat and me in equal measure. From my perspective, her impromptu strip teases were bearable but she was also clingy and neurotic. The arrangement seemed doomed but I had a fight to take care of, when all said and done.

Two of my last sparring sessions before the fight were with Dmitry Salita and John Duddy. Salita had a camera crew in tow making a documentary that would be called 'Orthodox Stance' and looked about 12 years old. Suffice to say he was a lot tougher than his visage despite the rapid capitulation to Amir Khan 6 and half years later. For whatever reason, our sparring session that day ended up on the cutting room floor which was a shame. Duddy, who had yet to make his pro debut, wasn't the quickest or most defensively savvy of fighters but punched like he had bricks in his gloves. He had the looks and personality to be a big star but couldn't quite cut it at the top level.

On July 4 - 8 days before the fight - I let myself down badly, getting slaughtered with Kat at a pool party in New Jersey. I hadn't touched a drop for 4 and a half weeks but found the Independence Day celebrations too much of a temptation in such an environment. The next day, I told myself that it wasn't a big deal. I was super fit and still had a week to get the toxins out of my system.

On the day of the fight, I spent the afternoon at Cammy's watching Leonard - Hearns 1 and the first Gatti - Ward clash. I had a light lunch of tuna and rice as my weight was good and I never went along with the notion that a fighter has to starve himself until he steps on the scales. At 5pm, Kat and I left for Gleason's where the show was taking place. Cammy, Stella and my friend, Guy, would come along later for moral support. I did wonder if fighting in a gym would lack the sense of ceremony that one found in the local Town Hall or a smoke filled working men's club but the upside was that the canvas would be utterly familiar to me.

We arrived at the venue and I weighed in at 154 pounds before going to look for Moe in the changing rooms. En route, I caught sight of my opponent. He looked like a skinny kid which immediately caused me to grow in confidence. John Douglas said, "I've seen him fight before. YOU can beat him...!" Still in the back of mind was the unspoken fear that the whole thing would prove to be a disastrous exercise in vanity by a 33 year old former heroin addict.

About half an hour before I was due on, Moe introduced me to a gentleman at ringside called Tommy Gallagher, who was accompanied by his wife that evening. Tommy was an East Coast boxing legend who had trained the likes of Vito Antuofermo, Doug DeWitt and Donny Lalonde. "If you knock this guy out in the first round tonight then maybe we can do something," said Moe. It was all a little bit surreal.

It was 8.30 pm when the time came for me to walk to the ring. As I mounted the steps, the MC heralded the presence of 'former 2 time world champion, Joey Gamache' in the house. I had called Joey earlier and was glad to hear he had made it. Hendrickson wore a blue vest with grey shorts and stomped his feet in some kind of premature victory dance ritual as he was announced to the crowd. When we came together in ring centre, he refused to make eye contact or touch gloves until coerced by the referee. It seemed like an awful lot of posturing before a punch had even been thrown.

The bell went and we sized each other up for 4 seconds before he threw a lead left hook which landed around the back of my head guard and a right hand that missed altogether. I slipped outside his jab and scored with a 4 punch combination then followed up with a 1-2/ left hook. The referee warned me for hitting on the break with another left hook and I extended my left hand in token apology. For the remainder of the round, I generally outboxed and outmanoeuvred the kid with a rhythm that didn't appear to be caked in 15 years of ring rust. He was switching stances but getting nailed from both and couldn't seem to figure out my movement as I darted in an out of range. In the corner, Moe and his assistant said to keep it up.

In the second round, the pattern changed as he caught me with a right hand early doors, then a rapid 'shoeshine' combination and another big right over the top.... then a right uppercut... then a right hook.... I was buzzed and responded like a 2 fight novice, blasting back at him. My head cleared and I drove him across the ring with a series of shots but now it was an alley fight and I never got back on track. The round was close but you'd have given it to him.

The third round was more of the same as we went back and forth on the inside. It takes a little longer than 4 months to get your ring fitness fully back after so long on the sidelines and the kid had a better engine than me. At 18 years old, he was damn well entitled to have.

The fourth round was all him as I basically ran out of gas and couldn't let my hands go with the same gusto. Gleason's was my turf and he was the outsider but, when the final bell sounded, I knew I had lost. We came back to the middle of the ring for the official verdict and I said, "Well done, son. You were too busy for me…" He gave a truculent shrug, suggesting that he had little interest in talking to some funny looking old white motherfucker with a strange accent. Following the traditional pregnant pause, the master of ceremonies confirmed that "HENDRICKSON" had won by a majority decision.

"Bullshit… You won that…!" reckoned John Douglas as I left the ring. A random guy in the front row agreed with him. "I'll do better next time," I offered. "I thought you did better this time," he shouted as I made my way to the dressing room. Moe said I was unlucky and it had been 'that close. "I'll see you on Monday," he added.

"No, I'm gonna' take a couple of days off, Moe. I'll be back Wednesday," I told him.

I had a shower and freshened up before returning to ringside and my small contingent of support. Despite being on the wrong end of the decision, I had received an inappropriately large trophy that looked more like first prize in the National Golden Gloves. Without thinking, I placed it next to Cammy's seat - symbolically between her legs - only for Kat to immediately snatch it away. They more or less hated each other.

As soon as we got outside the gym, I produced a can of 50 cent malt liquor from my kit-bag and downed it in one. Retrospectively, I can appreciate that any fighter who goes to a show with a can of 'Crazy Horse' in his bag probably has some kind of problem. Back in the 80s, I had been gutted every single time I lost but this felt completely different. Insert your own clichéd maxims about the triumph over adversity but I felt the same adrenaline that I had only previously experienced in victory. I was in the mood to celebrate

Cammy and Stella chose to go home so I hit the town with Kat, Niquae and Guy as subsequent events became a blur. To the best of my recall, we ended up in a popular bar called 'Time Out' on the Upper West Side. I was openly carrying my handsome trophy because it didn't fit in my bag and also because I was immensely proud of it. Although Kat and I had cooled on Niquae, there was a temporary amnesty resulting in risqué antics between the three of us as innumerable shots and beers were consumed. The last thing I could remember was some kind of conflagration over Kat's credit card being declined and the lights being turned on to prevent us from leaving. I can only assume that Guy must have paid the tab to avoid legal ramifications but anything thereafter remains a perfect blank.

CLOSURE

I woke up at 6am the next morning on a stationary subway train in a place called Throg's Neck which turned out to be in The Bronx. Inextricably linked in my hung-over brain with the bizarre name of the station was my own rather stiff neck, evidently incurred from sleeping in a sitting position. How far was I from Sunset Park and where were the girls..?

Had I really had my first fight in 15 years last night or was it a dream...? I looked down at my feet and was relieved to see the glorious purple and gold trophy lying horizontally on my bag, still in one piece. Carefully, I picked it up and held it a foot and a half in front of me, just to look at it. Engraved on the plaque affixed to the marble base were the words:

> 'GLEASON'S GYM 2003 AMATEUR BOXING
> RUNNER-UP'

Consolation trophies in amateur boxing always referred to the 'runner up' since loser doesn't have quite the same ring to it. In any case, I wasn't a loser. I had proven that to myself less than 12 hours ago and didn't care what someone else might think. There was a rocky road behind me and a rockier one ahead but I had rediscovered that sense of self that I couldn't find anywhere else. The simple truth was that I could find more value and nobility in losing a majority decision inside the squared circle than I would have done in winning the U.S lottery. That's the way I was wired and I was never going to change. Against all odds, the secondary school teachers had been proven right:

It's the taking part that counts.

ACKNOWLEDGEMENT

My mother, who told me not to do any of this but always encouraged me to write.

My darling Natalie for her love, loyalty and logistics.

Mick Guilfoyle, the best friend a man could have.

ABOUT THE AUTHOR

Ben Doughty

Ben Doughty is a boxing coach, journalist and pundit who lives in London. His all time heroes are Muhammad Ali and Sugar Ray Leonard and he is blessed with two beautiful sons, Joseph Cassius and Lucas Benjamin Doughty.

BOOKS BY THIS AUTHOR

Drink, Drugs, Birds & Boxing Volume 1

Printed in Great Britain
by Amazon